the girl & the fig Cookbook

More Than 100 Recipes from the Acclaimed California Wine Country Restaurant

Sondra Bernstein

Recipe Development by John Toulze

Photographs by M. J. Wickham

SIMON & SCHUSTER
NEW YORK LONDON
TORONTO SYDNEY

SIMON & SCHUSTER
Rockefeller Center
1230 Avenue of the Americas
New York, NY 10020

For information about special discounts for bulk purchases, please contact
Simon & Schuster Special Sales: 1-800-456-6798 or business@simonandschuster.com

Designed by Jeanette Olender
Manufactured in the United States of America

10 9 8 7 6 5 4 3 2 1

Library of Congress Cataloging-in-Publication Data
Bernstein, Sondra.
The girl & the fig cookbook : more than 100 recipes from the acclaimed California Wine Country Restaurant / Sondra Bernstein; recipe development by John Toulze.
p. cm.
1. Cookery, French. 2. Cookery—California—Sonoma.
3. Girl & the Fig (Restaurant) I. Title: The girl and the fig cookbook.
II. Toulze, John. III. Title.
TX719.B417 2004 641-5944—dc22 2003067323

ISBN 0-7432-5521-6

I strongly believe that in the restaurant business, you have two assets: your staff and your guests. I have been so fortunate to have both and the best of both. Many staff members, both past and present, have left a stamp on my business and my life. I have always believed in the importance of contribution. All of our staff members have contributed in their own personal way. They have given me a gift of themselves and an opportunity to spend time in this life with them. I have learned a lot from each of them, and many of their ideas and contributions are still found in the restaurant today. There are far too many to name here!

Without our supportive guests, the girl & the fig would have been a blink of the eye. You have been loyal, you have tried out our new creations, you have supported us through the economic highs and lows, and I am forever grateful to you.

a thank-you note

There are many people who I must thank and acknowledge for their inspiration, assistance, support, commitment, friendship, and existence. My dearest friend, alter ego, and brother in spirit is John. With admiration, I watched this man grow from a teenager to a young father with a lovely wife and angelic daughter. This is someone who has inspired me with his devotion, commitment, sense of pride, and fortitude. He has been my partner in crime (the crime of working too many hours in a day, too many hours in a week . . .). We have discovered food together in our own separate ways. John has taught himself the finer parts of cooking and developed an understanding of the relationships among food, temperature, and chemistry. Together we have shared a passion for the local products of Sonoma County. We have developed a relationship and an understanding about the sense of taste, as well as sharing our sense of place. He is the person who I can credit for taking my passion for food and translating it into something we can share with our guests. He has been able to commit to our concept of "country food with a French passion" and adopt it as part of his own. I have watched his style of cooking mature and his palate develop even further. We are lucky to have a symbiotic relationship about food. This doesn't happen overnight; this has been a process of many years of translation, experimentation, and trial and error. John, I thank you from the bottom of my heart—you have truly helped make my dreams come true. You have unselfishly encouraged my passion and often have been my muse.

Michael, without your help, this book would never have happened. Not only am I thankful for your assistance in the recipe testing and retesting, but I appreciate all of the help you have given from the beginning. You understand my passion for food quality, and your gentle touch and fantastic palate has always and will always be needed!

Many other people have participated in my search for soul, spirit, and sense of place. My brothers Ron and Ed and their families are supportive; their unconditional love made it possible for me to go out on my own in the wild world of the restaurant. My mother's artistic creativity and enthusiastic guidance have been extremely important and almost always appreciated. Her warmth, love, and support keep me going through some of the challenging times. My father is truly my biggest fan; he is a public relations firm of one. His encouragement and his ultimate faith and respect have led me to my career path. He has been my friend, adviser, nonjudgmental ear, resource for contacts and ideas, and one of my heroes.

Professionally, many people have inspired me. I'd like to thank my dear friend Gary, whose happy-go-lucky, even-keeled friendship has been solid. We have been lucky to share our culinary dreams and nightmares. Our friendship is truly precious and I hope he will always know this.

A heartfelt thank-you to Julie Higgins, whose amazing art now graces two of the restaurants and is an inspiration to me every day. Her creativity, sense of color, and sensual forms are so much a part of the girl & the fig that it wouldn't be the same without her magic.

I would like to thank Patti Britton, who is not only a good friend but an exceptional designer. She has created our logos and packaging and has contributed to the feel of the restaurant.

Without M. J. Wickham's beautiful photographs, this book would not be complete. She understood our vision and was able to incorporate our passion in her images.

Oh, yes, the recipe testers—a huge sympathetic thank-you (this was tougher than they thought and a lot less fun): my mom (who told me what she really thought!), my cousin Phyllis (who may have driven her butcher crazy), my dear friend Nancy Schultz (who smiled all the way through it and let us know when we used too much butter), and Allison's mom, Judy, who has been supportive and gracious from the very beginning. Thank you to my sister-in-law and dear friend Beverly, who tried to do the duck. To David, Nancy, Don, Tina, and Judy and all of the other recipe testers, thanks—I hope you got to eat some of your testing!

A special thanks to the following food enthusiasts who I have never met but who have had an influence on my culinary thoughts: Alice Waters, Sally Clarke, M.F.K. Fisher, Julia

Child, eGulleters, food bloggers, and all of the writers for the Wednesday food sections across the country.

Thank you to a very special literary agent, Cathy Fowler, whose guts and determination to follow her dreams have allowed me to fulfill mine. And thank you, especially, to my editor Laura Holmes, who has stepped out on a limb and taken a chance on me—the girl with the fig fetish.

contents

introduction

How do I define my culinary path to "country food with a French passion"? Years of searching have brought me to the heart of the valley of artisan food and wine, Sonoma. All my travels have narrowed the field for the place I belong—a place of soul and of spirit.

I want the girl & the fig to provoke a lasting memory so that someone will crave a fig salad or duck confit or a lavender crème brûlée long after they've visited the restaurant. I want to somehow be connected to someone else's food memories and be intrinsic to their sense of Sonoma.

The "French passion" refers to the sense of community that the French have in their eating and café life, which is convivial with family and friends, lots of conversation, the passionate sharing of ideas, and the long, leisurely meals and the lingering at the table. The cheese, the bread, the olives, the wine—oh, yes, the wine. Our cooking has roots in French cooking, but I believe those roots are in our passion about the raw ingredients combined with traditional techniques rather than what most people think of as French cooking. The parallel of the terroir of Sonoma Valley and Provence maintains a sense of place and captures my heart and inspires my ideas.

My Culinary Path

I have always considered myself lucky—not lucky the way some people win the lottery or find the perfect parking space; rather, I am lucky with food experiences. As I get older and think about my past, I see a sense of searching—searching for soul, searching for spirit, and searching for place. I have been fortunate enough to travel to faraway places and get a glimpse of other cultures, unusual traditions, beautiful landscapes, and interesting architecture. I have met fascinating people along the way and continued to pack away thoughts and memories of days gone by. What I remember most is a memorable meal or food experience.

In China, I ate "100-year-old eggs" and had to learn how to use chopsticks; I recall colorful wheeled food stalls full of unknown fare, each of us daring the other to try what was being offered. I remember toast after toast (and the morning-after effects of the previous night's rice wine drinking contests). On the way to Hong Kong, traveling by train, I watched as women waded through endless rice paddies, balancing baskets hung from poles across their shoulders.

In New York, I loved the smell of the roasted chestnuts on the corner of Fifty-fourth Street and Lexington (near Bloomingdale's) and the tangy sauerkraut and hot dogs on every corner.

In Tel Aviv, restaurants served little bowls filled with cucumbers, couscous, lentil salad, olives, fresh wet cheeses, roasted eggplants and peppers, hummus and tahini, accompanied by flatbread and pita.

In Kenya, we spent more time taking photographs of the animals than eating them. Even in the fanciest restaurants, the menu featured an array of vegetables prepared in unusual ways. I remember the baby goat put in my arms in Nairobi by a Masai tribesman. Cute as it was, I knew it was not really a pet and would probably be dinner in a few months.

In Tuscany, we dined in a small, elegant farmhouse restaurant. We tasted course after course, paired with wines, as someone's grandmother made pasta to order on a table in front of us in the middle of the dining room. Roasted meats, grilled vegetables, crusty breads, hard cheeses—we dined for hours.

In Florence, my first fig experience happened down a dark alley in a small café that sat twelve. We were served antipasti of fresh figs, rich Italian ham, extra virgin olive oil, and fresh cracked pepper. Light Italian music was playing in the background as the husband shouted in Italian to his wife.

In Paris, breakfast was usually a baguette with butter and a cup of hot chocolate. Lunch was a baguette with butter with a slice of cheese and ham, and dinner was a late-night revelation of braised stew, crisp duck, seared fish, and lots of cheese. Outside Paris, in the countryside, afternoons were spent sipping espresso and smoking cigarettes in cafés. Down in Monte Carlo by the beach, dinner consisted of thin pizzas topped with raw eggs.

In the Los Angeles area, the Beverly Hills Hotel was the place for a McCarthy salad, served with ranch dressing and tossed tableside by the pool. Westwood had me craving the chocolate layer cake with vanilla ice cream from Hamburger Hamlet, and Sunset Boulevard was home to Chinese chicken salad from Chin Chin. Fairfax and Third meant a greasy breakfast at Dupree's with at least one piece of cherry pie, and Sunday nights on Wilshire meant Ye Olde King's Head for lamb, mushy peas with mashed potatoes, and mint jelly.

At the Jersey Shore, White House was the place for a lunch pickup. Tuna subs, meatball sandwiches, and traditional hoagies served with chips and soda got us through a day of sunning and wave running. A trip to the Atlantic City boardwalk with my family meant an extra box of saltwater taffy to the pet-sitter.

In Philadelphia, where the food thing really began for me, a visit to the Reading Terminal was more about ogling and sniffing than it was about eating and tasting. Horn & Hardart meant tapioca pudding, and the best veal chop with sautéed escarole could be found at Dante & Luigi's on South 10th Street. A Milan salad could not be made properly without Baco-Bits, and a trip to Wawa was a waste without a pack of Tastykakes—peanut butter Tandy Takes or Butterscotch Krimpets. A trip to the Philadelphia art museum meant lunch at the museum café, and Sunday brunch was either jambalaya and spicy okra martinis at Nola's or bagels and lox at Hymie's. My brother Michael's birthday was usually a lobster dinner at Bookbinder's, his favorite, and after a late-night partying session on South Street, a Philly cheesesteak at Geno's was a necessity. After a day of playing tennis at the Green Valley Country Club, tangerine water-ice from Overbrook's was a thirst quencher.

In Santa Fe, I adored the smell of piñon wood coming out of the chimneys as I walked down the narrow sidewalks toward Café Pasquale, longing for the huevos rancheros served at the round communal table in the middle of the dining room. Fresh corn tortillas, tomatillo salsa, and black beans with adobo were my favorites.

At a Giants baseball game at PacBell Park, I have no idea who was playing but I remember the garlic fries: the smell, the taste, the texture. Deciding which restaurant to visit in San Francisco is difficult, but meze and warm pita from Kokkari, spicy green beans in black bean sauce from House of Nanking, dim sum from Yank Sing, or lettuce cups from Betelnut top my list.

In Chile, I wandered the aisles of the crowded Santiago marketplace, dazzled by the bright colors of the produce, breathing in the aromas of fresh cheese, and dodging live

chickens and roosters. Further south in Chile, we ate crêpes with fresh berries and cream while the rain came down in buckets.

In Mexico, the Guadalajara marketplace was filled with tropical fruits and large rotisseries roasting goats and pigs. The sounds of men and women cooing, cawing, heckling, and shouting out their wares and prices competed with the sounds of wild dogs barking and the cockfights hidden in the back.

At camp on Long Lake, Maine, I hated the fried chicken but loved the s'mores made with graham crackers, Hershey's chocolate, and marshmallows. I remember the secret canoe trip to Mario's Pizza for the most incredible chocolate chip cookies ever!

In Puerto Rico, tamales were sold in baskets outside the markets, and a taxicab driver took us to his favorite lunch spot, where we dined on Spanish rice, refried beans, shredded lettuce, and bad tomatoes. On the other side of the island, a cream-filled pastry brightened a stormy day of sightseeing in the rain. My time at Dorado Beach as a kid reminds me of sugar-glazed doughnuts and peanuts.

In Hawaii, with limited funds and an excess of time, I ate fruit from the trees and vegetables from someone's garden—whose, I don't know. I can barely see faces, but I remember the ripe papaya dripping juice down my chin and the fresh coconut out of the shell.

In Florida, I was torn between the sweet potato fries at Joe's Stone Crab and the garlic crabs served on newspapers at The Crab House.

On Tilghman Island, on the Chesapeake Bay, the trip was not complete without a family-style meal of fried chicken, baked ham, big bowls of succotash, mashed potatoes, and creamed corn, or without a stop in St. Michaels for Miss Sylvia's steamed crabs, Cheddar cheese, and pickles from The Crab Claw.

The Caribbean islands may remind most people of white sands and clear blue waters—but me, I am reminded of conch and papaya in St. Martin, rum and Diet Cokes in Curaçao, and fresh lobsters right off the boat, grilled on the beach in Anguilla.

My life has been a series of food memories, dining experiences, and eating rituals. I have found my soul, my spirit, and my sense of place through each nourishing bite, lingering flavor, and aromatic scent. I know that I cannot leave my food mecca without eating another steamed artichoke, steamed blue crabs, hearts of palm out of the can, fresh lichee nuts, warm challah bread, Tachinelli's white pizza, Santa Rosa plums, corned beef special with Thousand Island dressing and cole slaw, Osake's martini prawns, three dozen Hog Island oysters, Winchester Gouda cheese and fresh figs, roasted figs, grilled figs, figs with prosciutto, figs with goat cheese, figs with honey, figs with balsamic reduction, figs with Point Reyes Original Blue, and the girl & the fig Grilled Fig Salad.

the girl & the kids

It was important from the beginning that the girl & the fig would be a child friendly restaurant. It would be a place where a family could come and have a meal away from home with the kids and know that they would have a good time. We don't have a kid's menu, but on at least five occasions we have been critiqued by the French fry reviewers (ages three to six) as having the best fries (matchstick frites as we call them) ever! There are a handful of kids who I have watched grow up. There is Zoë (whom I often called Cloe), Olivia, and Hanna, and another Hanna and her new brother. There is Simon and Gabriel and Sienna and Gemma. There is Lilly and Riley and Michael and Blake and Kate and "my favorite raspberry girl" and "the twirling dancing girl." There are many, many more.

These are the kids who over the years left me with fantastic pictures with crayons on the table paper, little homemade cards, big hugs and wet kisses. These are the kids who peered over the counter to watch the chefs create their magic. These were the kids who took the toys home from the toy basket but brought a new one the next time to add to the collection. These are my favorite guests!

the girl & the staff

As I have told the staff many times, "A restaurant is only made of wood, bricks, cement, and glass; it is the people in it who create the experience and make the restaurant!" This is part of our training and this is what I believe. Every person who has worked at the girl & the fig has made a contribution in some form. These are the people who make it look easy but deal with the hard stuff, the day-to-day, the quality, the consistency, the smile, the knowledge, and the attitude!

I have been fortunate to have had many staff members stay with us over time, and they

have become my second family. I have watched them get married and have children. I have met many of their families and friends. I have seen what this experience has done for them and I know how much I have learned in turn. I have celebrated their joys, embraced their successes, and shared their sorrows. These are the people who have made the girl & the fig what it is today.

The Bridge Between Food & Service

The Passionate Fig Tenders

There is very little sense in being passionate alone. In the restaurant business, your food may become your art, but without a bridge between kitchen and guest, there may as well be a fast-food window. Our restaurant general managers are responsible for translating the passion that we create in our concept and our food and for teaching our staff to bring it to our guests. Gary and Dustin are there day to day specifically to ensure concept translation and guest satisfaction. They maintain an atmosphere that in some way enhances and enriches the lives of people with whom we come in contact. They focus on two areas. One is the work environment that our team of managers creates for our staff, and the other is the guest experience. The more passionate our staff is, the more they are willing to gain the knowledge necessary to do their jobs. We hope that the personality of each person who works at "the fig" shines through to our guests and to one another.

As for our guests, we are fortunate. Most people who walk through our doors are willing to let us take them on a journey. From the ambience of the restaurant to our cuisine to our distinctive Rhône wine list, it is our hope that each person leaves our doors in some way fulfilled, not just full! For the girl & the fig is a whimsical dining experience for guests and an enchanted lifestyle for those of us providing the experience.

A Note from Executive Chef John Toulze

For most of my life I have lived in the Sonoma Valley and have tried to take advantage of all that it has to offer. It is a place of great wealth and abundance in culture, history, agriculture, arts, and inspiring individuals. Sonoma is so fertile that it seems you need only to come here to be fruitful in your endeavors. Whether it is tending the numerous vineyards and organic farms or chasing your passion in art or life, Sonoma offers those who spend time within its enchanting hills more than any other area I know.

It is because of these blessings, or perhaps just fate, that I chose Sonoma to live my dream in which food takes center stage. For those who have had the opportunity to visit Sonoma, it is hard not to come in contact with the simplicity of life there. It is this simplicity and overwhelming quality of life that I have always tried to put into our food and is the centerpiece of my approach to cooking. I have never considered myself anything but a cook who is blessed with the ability to use the world's greatest produce, fish, cheese, meat, and

wine. It is a humbling experience to work with ingredients that individuals have poured their souls into; who am I to change the integrity of that ingredient? The best I can do is transport it to the plate in its truest form.

It is because of this philosophy, and once again fate, that I found my best friend and boss, Sondra. She will say that she found me and I don't mind that, but it is certainly not the case. There are very few times in life when you meet someone with whom you have little in common but understand everything that person is trying to achieve. Sondra is the single most inspirational and talented person I have ever worked with, and the clarity of her vision for the restaurants still astounds me to this day. I have often questioned her at the beginning of a project and at the end the only question that remained was why I ever questioned her in the first place. Whether it was the colors in the original restaurant, the "Rhône Alone" wine list, or even the name, Sondra has a talent that I have grown to appreciate. Together we have set out on a journey to follow our passions and share them with so many who have given us the opportunity to serve them.

The girl & the fig is the canvas on which we work; our tools are simple and goals humble. Food with integrity, a workplace for friends and family, and a restaurant that hopefully represents the best of our community: true, simple, and respectful of the earth and all it has to offer. I look forward to serving you!

the girl & the fig Cookbook

No greater thing is created suddenly, any more than a bunch of grapes or a fig. If you tell me that you desire a fig, I answer you that there must be time. Let it first blossom, then bear fruit, then ripen.

EPICTETUS

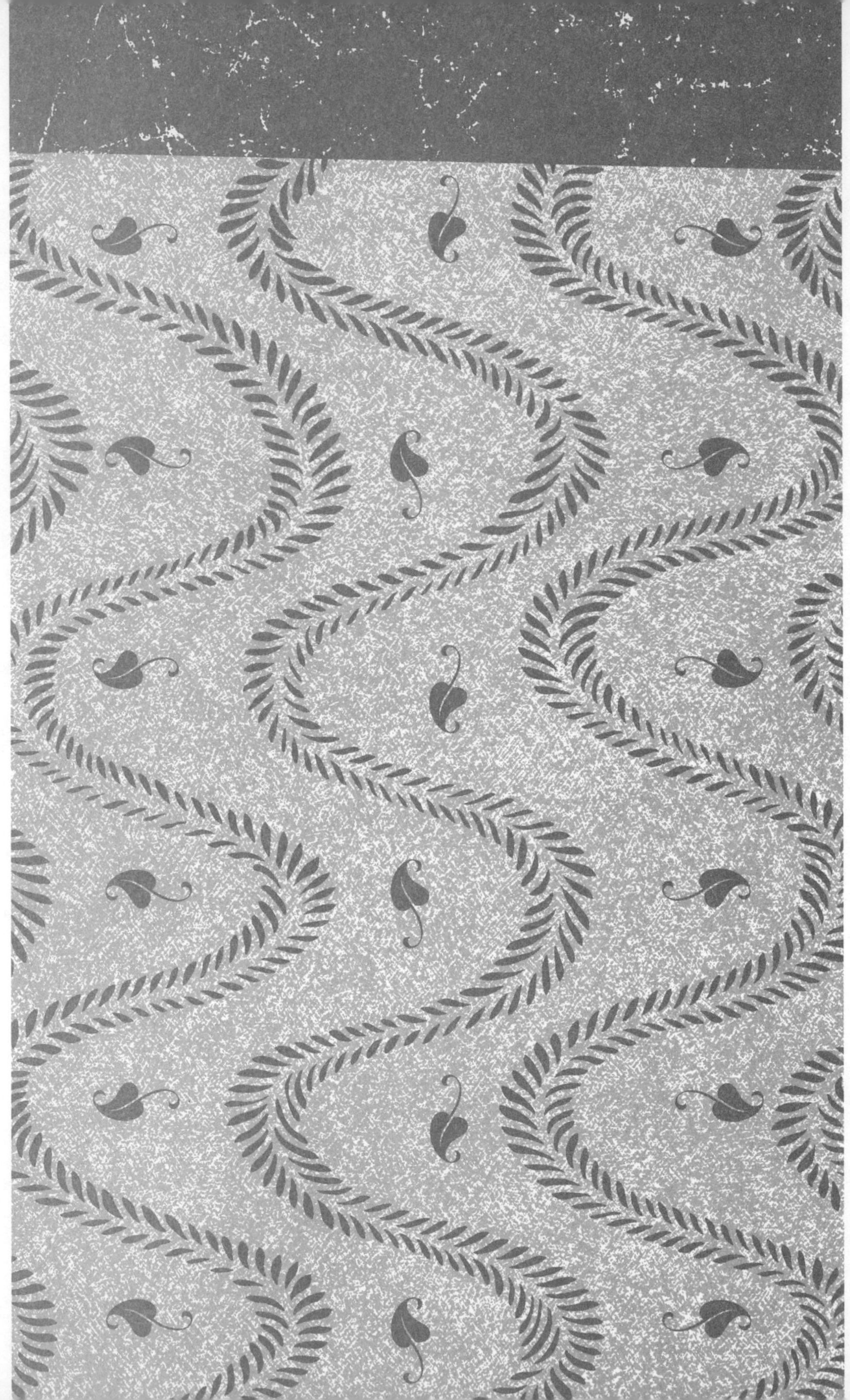

the pantry

Blended Oil
Herb Mix
Simple Syrup
Brown Butter
Crème Fraîche
Roasted Red Peppers
Mushroom Stock
Chicken Stock
Lobster Stock
Veal Stock

The Pantry Ingredients

The ten basic recipes in this section are used throughout the book. It will be helpful to have many of them on hand at all times. These are the ingredients we recommend you have on hand when cooking from this book. With our restaurant mentality, we use them frequently and prep them ahead in large quantities. For home use, depending on how often you cook, it will be helpful to have them in your refrigerator and on your pantry shelves.

Garlic
Shallots

Tarragon
Thyme
Sage
Parsley

Leeks
Fennel
Onions
Carrots
Celery

Kosher salt
White pepper
Black pepper

Herbes de Provence
Lavender
Capers
Caperberries
Olives

Dijon mustard
Whole-grain mustard

Extra virgin olive oil
Olive oil
Canola oil

Red wine vinegar
Champagne vinegar
Balsamic vinegar

Red wine
White wine
Pernod
Port
Sherry

Unsalted butter
Pancetta
Bacon
Prosciutto

The Flavor Enhancers

Balsamic vinegar is wine vinegar aged in small wood barrels in Modena, Italy. It is earthy in flavor and sweet in aroma. There are varying degrees of balsamic vinegar that depend on its age. The finest balsamic vinegars have been aged a minimum of twelve years. They take on a sweet sensation with a hint of sourness.

Bouquet garni is used throughout the book in recipes for soups, stocks, and sauces. Our basic bouquet garni consists of 3 to 4 thyme sprigs, 3 to 4 parsley sprigs, ½ teaspoon black peppercorns, and a bay leaf. Depending on the recipe, John adds 1 to 2 tarragon sprigs. Wrapping a bouquet garni in an outer leek leaf adds a bit more flavor, but a cheesecloth bundle wrapped with twine works just as well and even better for a shorter cooking time.

Capers in small amounts add a lot of flavor to a sauce, vinaigrette, or salad. Capers are buds from the caper bush that are picked before they flower. They are sun-dried and either pickled or salt brined. Our Liberty Duck Breast with Capers, Olives, and Herb Pan Sauce (page 136) is a fantastic large plate that uses the capers almost as a crust for the duck. Some of the capers fall into the pan sauce. The **caperberry,** also from the caper bush, is the mature fruit, slightly larger than a grape and generally pickled with their stems on. They have a less intense flavor than the caper and are crunchy and crisp. I use them as a garnish for a martini or Bloody Mary.

Definitely my favorite flavor enhancer, **fennel** is the ingredient I am most likely to grab off the prep table to nibble on while the guys are working. Eaten raw, anise is a great snack. Cooked fennel will do what celery does with the added benefit of the subtle licorice flavor. Fennel bulbs vary in size, and we use leftover scraps in our stocks. The fennel fronds, or "hair" as I call them, are used in our Apricot-Cured Salmon (page 38) or as a garnish for our Fig Leaf–Wrapped Rainbow Trout (page 122).

We use **garlic** in at least 70 percent of our recipes. Most often minced garlic is quickly sautéed in the pan as a flavor starter. We rarely use raw garlic, as the pungent odor and flavor will overpower the other elements. Roasted garlic is my favorite form of this luscious bulb. The sharp flavors of garlic are removed during roasting and a mellow, subtle essence is all that remains.

The girl & the fig **herb blend** consists of thyme, parsley, and sage. We chop one bunch of each and blend them together for our mise en place.

Herbes de Provence and **lavender** are typical flavors in southern France. If you want to make your own mix of herbes de Provence, your blend should include basil, fennel seed, lavender, marjoram, rosemary, sage, and thyme. When using lavender in recipes, be careful of its strength. If your lavender is overly strong in aroma, you may want to cut back just a tad. We use these herbs conservatively to achieve a subtle layer of aromatics and essence, not a punch.

Leeks are what I call the elegant onion. Long and lean, elegant in flavor and form, leeks give an additional layer of flavor that the onion cannot. Leeks are a mainstay of our cooking; baby leeks have a more delicate and aromatic essence. Sautéed with fennel, leeks are the foundation for our Pernod-scented mussel broth. Braised, they are a fantastic side dish for grilled fish; chopped, leeks end up in many of our soups and sauces.

Mustard is one of the many items that for me bridge Sonoma and Provence. When I see the wild mustard in the vineyards I daydream of France. As an ingredient, mustard adds an essence of astringency, tartness, and deep tones to every dish. We use both traditional Dijon mustard and whole-grain mustard in our vinaigrettes and in our cooking. Dijon mustard is ground mustard seeds blended with white wine and spices and smoothed out to a creamy paste. Whole-grain mustard is similar to Dijon except that the seeds are kept whole.

We greet our restaurant guests with a small bowl filled with our house-marinated **olives** (page 27). These are the perfect nibble to enjoy with an apéritif as our guests peruse the menu. Our blend is a combination of Lucque (my favorite), Picholine, Niçoise, and Nyons olives. We add caperberries, olive oil, thyme, and lemon zest and toss everything together. We also use our olive mixture in many of our menu items: they grace our Simple Salad (page 88) and our cheese plates.

Interestingly enough, olives all start out green—the green olives are simply not ripe. As they ripen on the tree, olives slowly turn shades of tan, reddish brown, and eventually black. The darker the olive, the higher its oil content and the richer its flavor. Olives are harvested in the fall after a long hot summer and are either brine cured or dry cured. Olives right off the tree are not edible—they have a horrible bitter flavor that sticks in your mouth for a while. Brine-cured olives are moist and smooth whereas dry-cured olives are wrinkled with a bolder flavor.

The **Lucque** olive is bright green and has a graceful curved shape. It is full-bodied and meaty. The **Niçoise** is a tiny, round, light brown olive that is brine cured. It is tender with a lovely subtle flavor. The **Nyons** has been dry cured in the sun and rubbed with olive oil. It is a small, greenish-black olive with bold and slightly bitter flavors. The **Picholine** is not as small as a Niçoise or as large as a Lucque. It is pale green and somewhat long in shape. This is a brine-cured olive with a crisp, mild, and nutty flavor.

Extra virgin olive oil is the first pressing of newly harvested olives (or fresh olive juice). This oil has been made with olives that are generally cold pressed within 24 to 36 hours of harvest. It is called extra virgin because it has not been filtered and it is the nectar of an olive. The flavor varies, based on the variety of the olive and its degree of ripeness. We rarely cook with extra virgin olive oil. Some recipes require this special flavor, but in most dishes we want a more subtle flavor with the velvety texture that olive oil imparts. This is a good product with full flavor and is not as expensive or robust as extra virgin. It may be used in our recipes that call for simple olive oil.

There are many types of **onions** available. Our everyday onion is a mild yellow onion. We use red onions, grilled and sliced, for our burgers. We like the mild flavor and crisp texture of the cipollini onion in a braised dish and the sweetness that a spring Vidalia or a Maui onion lends to a soup. Pearl onions are a pain to peel, but they are essential to our coq au vin. A quick rinse under some warm water will remove some of the intense flavor of onions and a quick chill in the refrigerator will bring fewer tears while chopping.

Pancetta is Italian bacon, cured with salt and spices. It has not been smoked and thus has a milder flavor than American bacon. When pancetta is slowly sautéed, it releases its fat. This fat is fantastic to use for grilling, as in our Grilled Fig Salad (page 98), and for sautéing garlic and/or shallots. Pancetta crisps up nicely and is a terrific garnish for pasta dishes and salads.

Parsley Once thought of as a typical restaurant garnish for just about every dish, parsley is an aromatic herb and very versatile in cooking. There are two types of parsley that we use, curly and Italian, but we almost always use Italian parsley because of its stronger, peppery flavor.

Pepper is a big part of our seasoning. Unless noted, we use black pepper. We start with whole peppercorns and grind them in a small spice grinder. We do this about every two days to keep the flavor fresh and sharp.

Rosemary will take over your garden if you let it, giving off a distinctive pinelike aroma.

We don't often use rosemary in our cooking, but occasionally a sprig of rosemary with roasted potatoes or as a skewer for figs will add just the right dimension of flavor to a dish.

Sage is a pretty herb with a pungent, slightly bitter flavor. On its own it has a very distinct taste, but when melded with thyme and parsley, there is a nice balance of flavors.

In our everyday cooking we use **kosher salt.** It is additive free and coarse grained. We season generously with salt, knowing that it really does sharpen the flavors of most food. Most recipes in this book end with "season with salt and pepper" or "adjust the seasoning."

The flavor of **shallots** is a cross between that of garlic and onions but is much more sophisticated than either one. Shallots vary in size and the smaller baby shallots have a more subtle flavor. Shallots are used in virtually all our sauces and dressings. They season the oil of an ingredient about to be pan-seared and add a spark to a citrus sauce.

Many people warn against overusing **tarragon;** they recommend using it sparingly and not with other herbs. We don't heed that advice. For us, tarragon's subtle, delicate flavor not only adds an anise-like aroma, but its acidic (slightly tart) properties will often balance out the seasoning of a dish.

Thyme is a woodsy, spicy, and earthy herb. As the thyme ages a bit, the stem becomes brittle and the leaves will easily brush off. When lemon thyme is available, it is everything that thyme is with a citrus scent and flavor.

Blended Oil

MAKES AS MUCH AS YOU WANT

We use blended oil for just about every recipe. Even plain olive oil, which we use here, can be very strong and in many recipes will overpower the dish, so we dilute the flavor with canola oil. This blend will be subtle and not overwhelm the other flavors in the dish.

1 part olive oil, such as Critelli (see Sources, page 252)
3 parts canola oil

Simply combine.

Herb Mix

MAKES AS MUCH AS YOU WANT

This is the ratio that we use in our restaurant herb mix. When all three of these herbs are called for in a recipe, it will simplify your cooking to have the mix on hand.

1 part fresh Italian parsley
1 part fresh thyme
1 part fresh sage

Chop and combine.

Simple Syrup

MAKES 1 CUP

1 cup sugar | **1 cup water**

Combine the sugar and water in a saucepan and bring to a simmer, stirring occasionally to dissolve the sugar. Remove from the heat and cool. Refrigerate until needed.

Brown Butter

MAKES ABOUT 1 CUP

¾ pound (3 sticks) unsalted butter

Heat the butter over medium heat in a small, heavy-bottomed saucepan. (The butter will melt and begin to simmer.) Carefully ladle off about ½ cup foam and allow the butter to continue to simmer. (The milk solids in the butter will eventually sink to the bottom of the pan.) When the butter begins to turn a deep golden brown and smells nutty, remove it from the heat and strain through a chinois or a fine-mesh sieve. (You may want to strain the butter twice to remove all the solids.)

Crème Fraîche

Makes $1\frac{1}{4}$ cups

1 cup heavy cream

2 tablespoons buttermilk

Mix the cream and buttermilk together in a plastic container. Cover the container with a layer of cheesecloth and secure with string or a rubber band. Leave the container out at room temperature for approximately 3 days or until the consistency becomes similar to that of sour cream. Refrigerate for up to 3 weeks.

Roasted Red Peppers

Makes $1\frac{1}{2}$ cups

These peppers are handy to have in the refrigerator. Tossed in olive oil and kept in a jar, they add zip to a recipe or can be used as a colorful garnish.

4 red bell peppers

1 tablespoon olive oil

Roast the peppers on all sides on a grill or under a broiler until the skin is well charred, about 3 minutes. Put the peppers in a container, cover with plastic wrap, and refrigerate until cool. Peel and seed the peppers and slice lengthwise. Toss with olive oil and refrigerate until needed.

Mushroom Stock

Makes 8 cups

- 2 tablespoons blended oil (page 7)
- 1 onion, chopped
- 1 carrot, peeled and chopped
- 2 celery stalks, chopped
- 4 leeks, green and white parts, chopped
- 1 tablespoon chopped fresh thyme
- 1 tablespoon chopped fresh sage
- 2 pounds mushrooms and stems, chopped
- 3 tablespoons minced garlic
- 5 dried morel mushrooms

In a heavy-bottomed stockpot, heat the oil and sauté the onion, carrot, celery, and leeks until the onion begins to brown, about 5 minutes. Add the thyme and sage. Add the chopped mushrooms and garlic and cook until the mushrooms are golden brown.

Cover the mixture with 10 cups cold water and mix in the dried mushrooms. Bring to a boil, lower the heat, and simmer for 1 hour. Strain and refrigerate.

Chicken Stock

Makes 2 quarts

- 1½ pounds chicken feet
- 5 pounds chicken necks
- 1 carrot, roughly chopped
- 2 onions, roughly chopped
- 2 celery stalks, roughly chopped
- ½ cup white wine
- 1 bay leaf
- 2 teaspoons black peppercorns
- 5 sprigs fresh thyme
- 4 sprigs fresh Italian parsley
- 1 teaspoon minced garlic

Preheat the oven to 450°F.

Roast the chicken parts in a roasting pan until brown, while in a separate roasting pan, roast the vegetables until slightly browned. Put the chicken and vegetables into a heavy-bottomed stockpot.

Heat up both roasting pans on the stovetop and deglaze each with 1 cup wine. Add the wine to the stockpot. Add the bay leaves, peppercorns, thyme, parsley, and garlic to the stockpot with 1½ gallons water. Bring to a boil, then reduce to a simmer. Cook on low heat for 4 hours. Strain the stock and refrigerate.

Lobster Stock

Makes 6 cups

- 3 pounds lobster bodies
- 2 tablespoons blended oil (page 7)
- ½ head celery, roughly chopped
- 2 medium onions, roughly chopped
- 1 large carrot, peeled and roughly chopped
- 1 fennel bulb, roughly chopped
- 1 teaspoon saffron threads
- ½ cup tomato paste
- 2 cups white wine
- ½ cup Pernod
- 4 garlic cloves, crushed
- 2 bay leaves
- 1 teaspoon black peppercorns
- 1 gallon chicken stock (page 11) or water
- salt and pepper

Preheat the oven to 350°F.

Place the lobster bodies on a baking sheet in the oven and roast for 15 minutes or until they are bright red. Set aside.

Heat the oil in a large heavy-bottomed stockpot and sauté the celery, onions, carrot, fennel, and saffron until the vegetables are lightly browned, about 5 minutes.

Add the tomato paste and cook for 2 minutes or until the tomato paste sticks to the bottom of the pot.

Add the white wine and Pernod.

Reduce the white wine mixture by half and add the lobster bodies, garlic, bay leaves, peppercorns, and chicken stock. Bring to a simmer and cook for 1 hour.

Strain the stock and reduce to 6 cups. Season with salt and pepper to taste.

Veal Stock

Makes 4 quarts

3 onions, roughly chopped
2 celery stalks, roughly chopped
2 carrots, peeled and roughly chopped
¼ cup whole garlic cloves, peeled
10 pounds veal bones
½ cup tomato paste
1 cup red wine
4 bay leaves
2 teaspoons black peppercorns
6 fresh thyme sprigs
8 fresh Italian parsley sprigs

Preheat the oven to 350°F.

In a heavy-bottomed stockpot, cook the onions, celery, carrots, and garlic until caramelized, 4 to 5 minutes.

In a roasting pan, roast the bones until brown, about 1 hour. Remove the bones, smear them with the tomato paste, and roast for another 10 minutes. Remove the bones and put the roasting pan on the stovetop over medium heat. Deglaze with the red wine. Add the bones to the stockpot. Add the wine, bay leaves, peppercorns, thyme, parsley, and 10 quarts water.

Bring to a boil, reduce the heat, and let simmer for at least 6 hours, skimming every 20 minutes. Strain, let cool, and refrigerate.

apéritifs and cocktails

the girl & the fig Martini (sweet and fruity)
the fig & the girl Martini (tart and bitter)
Fig Royale
Provence Martini

Stimulating the Appetite and Adding Flavor with an Apéritif

Apéritifs are wines or liqueurs that help stimulate the appetite. They may be infused with herbs or fruits. We carry a wide variety at the restaurant and encourage our guests to give them a try.

Anise-flavored apéritifs include **Ricard, Pernod, pastis,** and **Herbsaint.** The differences lie in their secret recipes of herbs and spices. These drinks are traditionally served with a side of ice, a pitcher of water, and a sugar cube. This is an "interactive" apéritif that allows guests to create their own recipes with sugar, water, and licorice flavor.

Campari is an apéritif made in Italy. Bright red, it has a spicy bitter flavor that is herb based. Campari is delicious served straight, on the rocks, or with club soda and a lemon twist.

Dry vermouth is a fortified wine infused with a secret recipe of herbs, spices, and alcohol. Vermouth has subtle flavors and floral and herbal aromas. It may be served chilled or over ice with a lemon twist.

Figoun is a wine-based apéritif infused with figs, oranges, vanilla, and angelica, slowly macerated together to create this unusual blend. Produced in Provence, Figoun has a rich fruitiness that is very refreshing served over ice. Figoun can be served chilled or with sparkling wine.

Lillet blanc is a wine-based apéritif made with white grapes and orange and lemon brandies to which quinine is added. This mixture is then aged in oak barrels. Lillet blanc is best served chilled or over ice with an orange slice.

Suze is a sharp and bitter apéritif made from a wild plant that grows in the mountains in France. The root of the gentian is steeped with a secret recipe of other herbs and spices. This unusual apéritif is an acquired taste. We serve it chilled, over ice, or with tonic.

Pineau des Charentes is a luscious, gold-amber-colored liquid made from a blend of white or red grapes from the Cognac region of France. Pure unfermented grape juice and

RICARD · RICAR
DEPUIS 1932
RICARD
45
750 ml
FRANCE
PASTIS DE MARSE
RICARD

Cognac are mixed and aged for at least a year. Pineau des Charentes has the sweet scent of sun-dried raisins, the flavors of soft spices, and fruity tones. Served slightly chilled, Pineau des Charentes complements any cheese or charcuterie platter.

Sparkling wine is always a fantastic apéritif, not only to stimulate the appetite but to encourage celebration. Our sparkling wines are always dry, crisp, and refreshing. Peach nectar, Figoun, or framboise are wonderful mixers that add a hint of sweetness to the sparkling wine.

Spirits That Add Flavor

Bonny Doon Framboise is an infusion of raspberry made by Bonny Doon Vineyard. It has an essence of ripe raspberries. This apéritif features the Morrison variety of raspberry, which has wonderful wild raspberry character. Extremely vibrant, this apéritif is intense and enticing. We use framboise in many of our signature drinks as well as in many of our recipes. Framboise is a great accompaniment to chocolate.

Figoun is a wine-based apéritif that is infused with figs, oranges, vanilla bean, and other fruits and spices. Figoun, produced in Provence, has a rich fruitiness and is deliciously refreshing served over ice with a twist of lemon. One of our specialty apéritifs is sparkling wine and Figoun with a twist of lemon.

Pernod is one of many licorice-anise, alcohol-based apéritifs. We use Pernod in many of our recipes. During the cooking process, the alcohol is cooked off and what remains is an element of sweetness and a hint of anise.

Dry vermouth is a fortified wine that has been infused with a secret recipe of herbs, spices, and alcohol. Dry vermouth works well when deglazing a pan, imparting a distinctive herbal flavor.

the girl & the fig martini (sweet and fruity)

Serves 1

¼ cup Feigling Vodka (fig-flavored vodka from Germany)
splash of Bonny Doon Framboise
fresh mint sprig

Fill a martini shaker with ice. Add the vodka and framboise and shake. Strain into a chilled martini glass and garnish with the mint.

the fig & the girl martini (tart and bitter)

Serves 1

¼ cup Feigling Vodka (fig-flavored vodka from Germany)
splash of Campari
fresh mint sprig

Fill a martini shaker with ice. Add the vodka and Campari and shake. Strain into a chilled martini glass and garnish with the mint.

Fig Royale

SERVES 1

1 ounce Figoun (see Sources, page 254)
sparkling wine
lemon twist

Pour the Figoun into a Champagne flute. Top with sparkling wine and garnish with a lemon twist.

Provence Martini

SERVES 1

1½ ounces Figoun (see Sources, page 254)
1 ounce vodka
splash of fresh lemon juice
splash of simple syrup
lemon twist

Fill a martini shaker with ice. Add the Figoun, vodka, lemon juice, and simple syrup. Shake well. Strain into a chilled martini glass and garnish with a lemon twist.

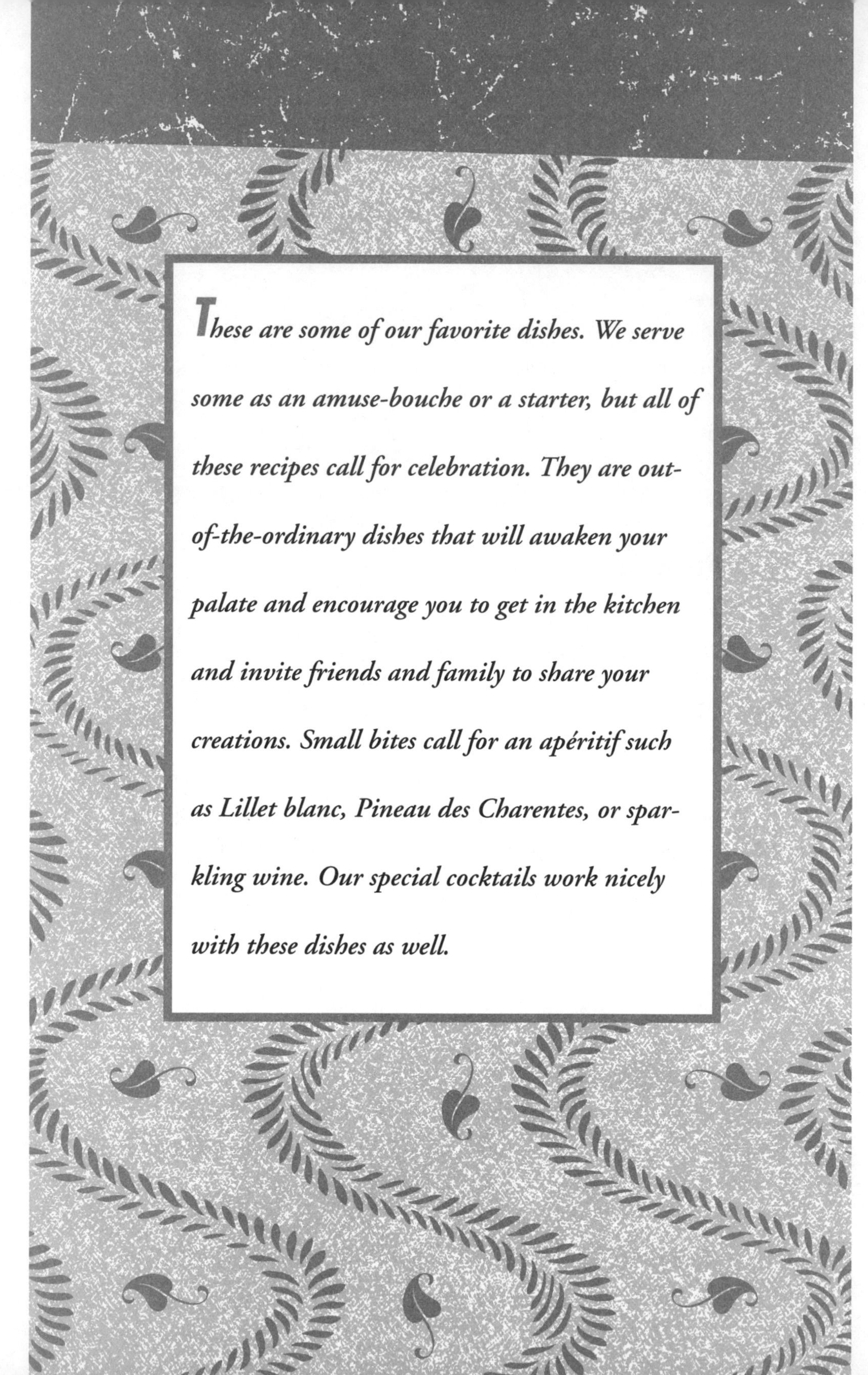

These are some of our favorite dishes. We serve some as an amuse-bouche or a starter, but all of these recipes call for celebration. They are out-of-the-ordinary dishes that will awaken your palate and encourage you to get in the kitchen and invite friends and family to share your creations. Small bites call for an apéritif such as Lillet blanc, Pineau des Charentes, or sparkling wine. Our special cocktails work nicely with these dishes as well.

a small bite

Heirloom Radishes with Anchovy Butter and Sea Salt
Herb-Marinated Olives
Fresh Figs with Fromage Blanc and Pine Nuts
Rosemary-Skewered Figs
Prosciutto-Wrapped Figs
Savory Goat Cheese–Stuffed Figs
Vella Cheese Crisps
Goat Cheese Fritters
Gougères with Wildflower Honey
Apricot-Cured Salmon
Pernod-Scented Mussels
Dungeness Crab Cakes
Polenta Cakes
Shrimp and Salmon Cakes
Asparagus and Onion Frittata
Garden Herb Tartlet
Fig, Prosciutto, and Roquefort Pissaladière
Chicken Liver Mousse
Duck and Mushroom Rillettes
Foie Gras Tourchon with Dried Fig Compote
Pork and Dried Cherry Pâté
Rabbit and Hazelnut Pâté with Pickled Figs
Crispy Sweetbreads

Heirloom Radishes with Anchovy Butter and Sea Salt

SERVES 6

A cold, crisp radish is my unqualified example of how important texture is to any dish: texture adds dimension to flavor. In this very simple recipe, the crunch of the radish is enhanced by the creaminess of the butter and the saltiness of the anchovies. The recent renewal of heirloom radish varietals has redefined this simple crudité.

1 pound assorted radishes (Easter Egg, Icicle, and Flambo varieties are ideal)
¼ pound (1 stick) unsalted butter
4 anchovy fillets, chopped
1 tablespoon minced shallots
1 tablespoon lemon juice
2 tablespoons chopped fresh Italian parsley
1½ tablespoons gray sea salt

Clean and trim the radishes in cold water. Combine the butter, anchovies, shallots, lemon juice, and parsley in a food processor and blend well.

Arrange the radishes on a plate and serve with a side of anchovy butter and a side of sea salt.

WINE PAIRING **Sparkling wine, Lillet blanc**

FOOD FOR THOUGHT *Serve this traditional crudité with other light bites including Shrimp and Salmon Cakes (page 44), Polenta Cakes (page 43), and Haricots Verts (page 173).*

my favorite radishes

Many types of radishes are available in seed form today. Here are a few varieties that we use on a regular basis.

EASTER EGG radishes are multicolored with shades of red, pink, purple, and white. They have a crunchy white flesh and a mild and sweet flavor.

WHITE ICICLE radishes are long and thin skinned. They grow up to 6 inches long and look like an icicle hanging from a shingle. These radishes are mild and flavorful and have a crisp texture.

FLAMBO or **FRENCH BREAKFAST** radishes are one of the most common available. These are a spring-summer radish. They are about 2 inches long and have an oblong shape with white-tipped red tops. These radishes are mildly spicy.

WATERMELON radishes are round with a white and hot pink flesh. They are spicy with a crunchy texture.

Herb-Marinated Olives

MAKES 4½ CUPS

This simple combination can be made with your favorite olives and herbs. Remove from the refrigerator about an hour prior to serving. These olives are wonderful to have on hand for snacking or for a cocktail party.

- 1 cup Lucque olives
- 1 cup Niçoise olives
- 1 cup Nyons olives
- 1 cup Picholine olives
- ½ cup caperberries
- ¼ cup lemon zest (thin strands)
- 1 bunch thyme, leaves removed
- ¼ cup extra virgin olive oil

In a large bowl, toss all the ingredients together.

Fresh Figs with Fromage Blanc and Pine Nuts

Serves 6

Cowgirl Creamery is a local dairy in Tomales Bay, just north of San Francisco. Among their very fine cheeses, the Fromage Blanc is exquisite. Cowgirl Creamery uses especially fresh organic milk from the Straus Family Dairy, not far from the cheese-making facility. Fromage Blanc can be substituted for cream cheese in just about any recipe and can be found in most specialty food markets. This pasteurized cow's milk cheese is just as fresh as cheese can be.

¾ cup Fromage Blanc
¼ cup honey
¼ cup pine nuts, toasted
12 fresh figs

Preheat the oven to 350°F.

Mix the cheese, honey, and toasted pine nuts in a bowl. Slice off the top third of each fig. Gently scoop out the fig flesh with a mellon baller. Fill each fig with the Fromage Blanc mixture. Roast the figs for 10 minutes and serve.

Wine pairing **Grenache**

Food for thought *If you have Fromage Blanc left over, add a spoonful to pasta dishes or omelets, or spread on toast with your favorite jam.*

the bounty

Five Fig Varieties

In general, I prefer dark-skinned figs, deep purple to almost black. They seem to have the most aromatic and intense flavors and are the ones I love to drape with prosciutto, drizzle with olive oil and freshly cracked pepper, and eat raw. The lighter-skinned figs are moist and tender on the inside but often the skin is tough and unpalatable. These figs make fantastic compotes and preserves. Because figs are so versatile, we make good use of them in season. They are eaten raw as an accompaniment to cheese or charcuterie, stewed for jams, roasted with vegetables and meats, baked with soft cheeses and eaten for dessert, and pureed for dressings, sauces, and syrups. The many varietals are important in preparing recipes. Throughout the book, I am not always specific about which fig varietals to use, because not all varietals are always available.

Following are the basic fig varieties we use during the fig season, though at times we may be fortunate enough to obtain a Celeste, Marseille, or Bordeaux fig as well.

Choose figs that are plump, fragrant, and firm, but that give to the touch. They should not be split or bruised. Figs usually ripen on the tree, but if they are not quite ripe, leave them out on the counter for a day or so and they should soften up.

ADRIATIC figs are medium sized with a green-yellow skin and strawberry-colored flesh. The skin is tough, but the flavors are luscious. We use this fig primarily for the jam in our Warm Fig and Thyme Crisp (page 216).

BLACK MISSION figs have purple-black skin and strawberry-colored flesh. They are small to medium sized and have a tender skin and an intense flavor. This is the fig we use in our Fig and Port Vinaigrette (page 99).

BROWN TURKEY figs are medium to large sized with a purple-brown skin and a pink-amber flesh. They are sweet and plump. We use them in our Grilled Fig Salad (page 98).

CALIMYRNA figs are medium sized with a golden skin and golden-ivory flesh. They have a nutty flavor and are very tender and delicate.

KADOTA figs have a yellow-green skin and amber-colored flesh. They are medium sized with a tough skin and are almost seedless with a high sugar content.

Rosemary-Skewered Figs

Serves 6

Many of our guests complain about the huge quantity of figs from their trees. These are folks who generally don't make preserves, and many of them are bored with figs after the first of the two harvests. We are often the lucky recipients of their fig harvest. During our busy season we can never have too many figs on hand and we have created some very simple recipes to use up the surplus.

12 fresh figs
twelve 3-inch-long rosemary sprigs
¼ cup extra virgin olive oil
salt and pepper

Preheat the oven to 350°F.

Skewer each whole fig on a rosemary sprig and drizzle with olive oil. Season with salt and pepper. Roast the figs for 10 minutes and serve.

Wine pairing **Mourvèdre**

Midnight purple rippled, fragrant skin
Concealing moist, succulent dampness within
A simple slit revealing sodden, seeded treasure
Teasing taste, affording temporary pleasure . . .
Your attributes by nature lovers sung
You resist my subtle probing tongue.
What effort will it take to spread apart,
Expose to lust your soft and sensuous heart . . .
The most delectable, the most divine
Consumed with golden blush of finest wine
Oh aphrodisiac, voluptuous, plump, intense
One morsel sweet envelops every sense
You lie before me, temptress at my table
Oh luscious fig, oh fecund fruit of fable.

BEVERLEY DIPLOCK, "MISSION IMPENETRABLE"

Prosciutto-Wrapped Figs

SERVES 6

We always tell John that he should be the president of the Pork Council because he loves just about every type of pork product. We benefit from cooking with bacon, pancetta, Spanish jamon, and prosciutto di Parma in many ways—mostly in flavor!

12 fresh figs, cut in half
12 slices prosciutto, sliced very thin
¼ cup extra virgin olive oil

Preheat the oven to 350°F.

Wrap the fig halves with the prosciutto and drizzle with olive oil. Roast the figs for 15 minutes and serve.

WINE PAIRING Grenache

Savory Goat Cheese–Stuffed Figs

Serves 6

Laura Chenel, one of the first artisan cheese makers in California, is legendary in Sonoma County. Not only does she make some of the finest goat cheeses around, she is an amazing person as well. These cheeses are reminiscent of some of the goat cheeses in France, where she learned her trade.

We have been using her chèvre in our Grilled Fig Salad (page 98) since we opened the restaurant. This is a superbly structured cheese, flavorful served at room temperature and also tremendous to cook with. This particular chèvre is creamy, very fresh tasting, and slightly tangy.

¾ cup goat cheese, softened
2 tablespoons chopped fresh basil
2 tablespoons chopped fresh sage
½ teaspoon sea salt
12 large fresh figs
2 tablespoons blended oil (page 7)

Preheat the oven to 350°F.

In a food processor, combine the goat cheese, basil, sage, and sea salt. Set aside.

Slice off the top third of each fig. Gently scoop out the fig flesh with a melon baller. Fill each fig with the goat cheese mixture. Replace the fig tops. Drizzle the figs with the oil. Roast the figs for 10 minutes and serve.

Wine pairing **Mourvèdre**

Food for thought *You can add a bit of fresh tomato or use other herbs and spices with the goat cheese mixture. Experiment with different ingredients to come up with your own recipe.*

Vella Cheese Crisps

MAKES 24 PIECES

These are quick and easy snacks and great garnishes for salads, pastas, and soups as well. While the crisps are hot, lay them inside a small bowl and the crisp will maintain a bowl shape as the cheese cools. We like to fill these bowls with our Roasted Baby Beet and Blood Orange Salad (page 96).

¾ pound Vella Dry Jack, finely grated (see Sources, page 252) (Parmesan may be substituted)

Preheat the oven to 350°F.

Divide the cheese into 6 equal portions. Spread evenly on a Silpat mat laid in a baking pan, forming a 6-inch circle for each portion. Bake for 7 to 9 minutes until lightly brown. Remove from the oven and let cool for 30 seconds before removing from the baking pan. Slice into quarters and serve.

WINE PAIRING **Carignane**

Goat Cheese Fritters

SERVES 6

We have tried making this fritter with many cheeses. A semisoft cow's milk cheese, a creamy fresh chèvre, and a triple crème will all taste delicious.

1 egg
6 tablespoons panko (dried bread crumbs may be substituted)
¾ pound goat cheese
2 cups canola oil for frying

Lightly beat the egg in a small bowl and put the panko in a separate bowl. Slice the cheese into small portions (about 1 ounce each) and dip into the egg. Dip the cheese in the panko bowl and coat well. Repeat with the other cheese slices.

On the stovetop, heat the oil in a small pan until it reaches 350°F. Deep-fry the fritters in about 2 inches of oil until they are light brown, 2 to 3 minutes per side. Serve immediately.

WINE PAIRING **Cinsault**

FOOD FOR THOUGHT *Serve these fritters with baguette slices and Fig and Olive Relish (page 161) or other savory accompaniments such as Roasted Tomato and Garlic Sauce (page 165) or Wild Mushroom Ragout (page 182). These fritters will also liven up a simple salad of field greens with Champagne vinaigrette (page 97).*

Gougères with Wildflower Honey

MAKES 25 GOUGÈRES

Our gougères are addictive. These delicate little cream puffs baked with cheese are best eaten when they first come out of the oven. Drizzle your favorite honey generously over the gougères; just don't count how many you eat before you serve them to your guests!

6 tablespoons unsalted butter
1½ teaspoons salt
¼ teaspoon cayenne
1 cup flour
5 eggs
½ cup blue cheese (we prefer Point Reyes Original Blue)
¼ cup wildflower honey

Preheat the oven to 350°F.

In a heavy-bottomed saucepan, bring 1 cup water to a boil along with the butter, salt, and cayenne. Boil the mixture until the butter melts and remove from the heat. Pour in the flour and beat the mixture for another minute with a wooden spoon to blend and bind the ingredients.

Return the pan to medium heat and continue to beat until the dough pulls away from the sides of the pan and holds together, about 2 minutes. Remove from the heat.

Make a well in the dough and break an egg into it. Beat with a wooden spoon to incorporate the egg. Repeat until 4 of the eggs are incorporated into the mixture and it is a smooth paste. Add the blue cheese and beat until smooth. Fill a large pastry bag with the mixture and refrigerate for an hour.

Butter a baking sheet or use a Silpat mat. Squeeze the dough into about 1-ounce puffs. In a small bowl, beat the remaining egg with 1 teaspoon water. Using a pastry brush, coat the top surface of each puff with the egg and water mixture.

Bake until the puffs are golden brown, 12 to 15 minutes. Let cool for a minute before serving. Drizzle with honey and serve.

WINE PAIRING Lillet blanc, Pineau des Charentes

Apricot-Cured Salmon

SERVES 6

Our house-cured apricot salmon is exquisite, and I always know when to expect it. After a few days of seeing the walk-in refrigerator filled with pans loaded with 10-pound cans of tomato paste, I know what is curing underneath. This salmon is not quite like what I remember eating every Sunday on a bagel at Hymie's deli on Montgomery Avenue in Narberth, Pennsylvania, but it's simply delicious. The aroma of very fresh fish is what makes this salmon so special, so be sure to use the freshest fish available.

- **½ cup dried apricots**
- **½ cup Pernod**
- **¼ cup kosher salt**
- **¼ cup sugar**
- **1 teaspoon black peppercorns**
- **2 fennel fronds**
- **1 pound salmon fillet (with skin)**

Place the apricots in a bowl of hot water, add the Pernod, and rehydrate for 20 minutes. Puree the apricots in a food processor. Mix the puree with the salt, sugar, peppercorns, and fennel fronds.

Cut a piece of cheesecloth large enough to cover the salmon. Place the cheesecloth in a large baking dish and lay the salmon skin side down on the cheesecloth. Cover the salmon evenly with the apricot-salt mixture and wrap it with cheesecloth.

Place another baking pan over the cheesecloth and weight it down with at least 3 pounds of pressure (you can use water jugs, tomato cans, or even books). Refrigerate for 48 to 72 hours.

Remove the weights and unwrap the salmon. Remove excess salt mixture from the salmon and pat dry. Slice very thin and serve.

WINE PAIRING **Sparkling wine or Roussanne**

FOOD FOR THOUGHT *Serve thin slices of Apricot-Cured Salmon with crisp endive leaves and crème fraîche. You can also serve it with herbed cream cheese and crackers; or use the salmon in an omelet with spring onions and fresh herbs; or make tea sandwiches with the salmon, cucumber slices, and unsalted butter.*

a real salmon fisherman

Ray, Bodega Bay

Ray is serious about salmon and John is serious about buying salmon from Ray. We know the fish was caught that morning and the price is always right. The pink salmon skin still glistens with sea salt when it arrives at the restaurant, and the aroma is light and fresh.

Ray is his own salmon company, which he calls Footloose, after the name of his boat. He catches the fish and then distributes it, so we often don't get our fish until eight or nine in the evening. Ray is a one-man show and I know he works very hard. We make decisions about our menu when Ray calls and says, "John, do you want some salmon?" He tells John the different weights of the salmon he has caught and John selects the ones he wants.

There is definitely something special about preparing and serving a meal when you know the source of the ingredients; it always tastes better.

Pernod-Scented Mussels

Serves 6

Some of my favorite essential ingredients used in French cooking include fennel, leeks, garlic, thyme, and black pepper. Many recipes throughout this book incorporate these ingredients in different combinations. This is one of those recipes.

Prince Edward Island mussels are tender and meaty, and slightly briny from the sea. Their flavor, combined with that of Pernod, white wine, and fennel, creates a melody of flavor.

- 3 pounds mussels (preferably Prince Edward Island)
- 2 tablespoons blended oil (page 7)
- 3 leeks, white parts only, thinly sliced
- 1 fennel bulb, sliced lengthwise in strips
- salt and pepper
- 1 tablespoon minced garlic
- 2 cups dry white wine
- 1/4 cup Pernod
- 2 teaspoons chopped fresh Italian parsley
- 3 teaspoons chopped fresh thyme
- 3 tablespoons unsalted butter

Clean the mussels under cold water, removing the beards and any dirt on the shell, and dry thoroughly.

Heat the oil in a large sauté pan and add the leeks and fennel. Season lightly with salt and pepper. Sauté until the leeks start to turn translucent, about 5 minutes. Add the garlic and mussels and stir well. Add the white winc and Pernod and cover the pan. Cook slowly over medium heat until the mussels start to open, 5 to 6 minutes. Remove the lid, add the herbs and the butter, and cook for 2 more minutes. Taste the sauce and adjust the seasoning as needed. (Mussels can hold saltwater inside, so be careful not to oversalt.)

Wine pairing **Viognier**

Food for thought *Serve the mussels with grilled French bread to soak up the juices. If you have any mussels left over, chill and serve on the half shell with Tarragon Aïoli (page 160).*

Dungeness Crab Cakes

Serves 24 as a small bite or 12 as a main course

Other than the Chesapeake Bay, there is no better place to eat crabs than northern California. When I saw my first Dungeness crabs in Bodega Bay, I couldn't believe how large they were. Not only were they gigantic, but the crabmeat was much more delicate than I expected.

When Dungeness season starts, we are ecstatic. Not only do we prepare this crab cake recipe but we also make Crab and Mushroom Chowder (page 80), add crab to omelets and quiche, and serve it in our Provençal Seafood Stew (page 79).

- **2 pounds cooked crabmeat (preferably Dungeness crab)**
- **½ cup Tarragon Aïoli (page 160)**
- **1 tablespoon Dijon mustard**
- **1 celery stalk, minced**
- **½ medium onion, minced**
- **1 teaspoon coriander, ground**
- **¼ teaspoon paprika**
- **¼ teaspoon Worcestershire sauce**
- **2 cups panko (dried bread crumbs may be substituted)**
- **1 tablespoon lemon juice**
- **salt and pepper**
- **½ cup Blended Oil (page 7)**

In a colander, drain as much moisture as possible from the crabmeat and pick through it, removing any pieces of shell. Mix the crab, aïoli, mustard, celery, onion, coriander, paprika, and Worcestershire sauce together in a large bowl. Adjust the consistency by adding panko. (The mixture should be semifirm.) Adjust the seasoning with the lemon juice, salt, and pepper.

Form the mixture into 24 cakes for a small bite or 12 cakes for a main course. Heat the Blended Oil in a medium sauté pan over medium heat and sauté the cakes until golden brown, 1½ to 2 minutes per side. Serve hot.

Wine pairing **Viognier or Marsanne**

Food for thought *Try these crab cakes with Celery Root Remoulade (page 160), Red Pepper Rouille (page 162), or fresh tomato Pistou (page 161).*

Polenta Cakes

Serves 6

Polenta (cornmeal) is a very versatile staple, and we use it in a variety of forms on our menu. The texture of coarse polenta adds another element to many dishes. Herbs can transform simple cooked polenta, as do savory items such as cheese or mushrooms.

4 tablespoons (½ stick) unsalted butter
1 teaspoon minced garlic
1 tablespoon chopped fresh Italian parsley
1 tablespoon chopped fresh thyme
2 teaspoons chopped fresh sage
3 cups heavy cream
salt and pepper
2 cups coarse polenta

nonstick cooking spray

Preheat the oven to 350°F.

Heat the butter in a saucepan over medium heat. Sauté the garlic until it turns golden brown. Add the herbs and mix well. Add 5 cups water and the heavy cream. Season with salt and pepper and bring the mixture to a boil. Whisk in the polenta and reduce the heat to a simmer. Cook, stirring frequently, until the polenta starts to pull away from the sides of the pot, 10 to 15 minutes. Adjust the seasoning.

Spray six 4-inch ramekins with nonstick spray and fill them with the polenta mixture. Bake for 15 minutes. Let cool slightly, remove from the ramekins, and serve.

Wine pairing **Cinsault**

Food for thought *Cut the polenta into wedges for a small bite and serve with Red Pepper Rouille (page 162) or Saffron Balsamic Essence (page 163). Polenta cakes can also be served as a side to a main dish such as Braised Beef Short Ribs (page 155). They can be easily grilled or pan-fried as well.*

Shrimp and Salmon Cakes

Makes 12 cakes for a small bite or 6 for a main course

We have been preparing shrimp and salmon cakes since 1998. Plump cakes of moist salmon bound with shrimp, these cakes are spiced up with a bit of jalapeño, cilantro, and chipotle powder.

- ½ pound salmon, skin removed, salmon cut into 1-inch cubes
- ½ pound shrimp, peeled, deveined, and chopped
- 1 teaspoon red wine vinegar
- 1 teaspoon soy sauce
- 1 teaspoon minced garlic
- ¼ green bell pepper, diced
- ⅓ jalapeño, diced
- ½ small onion, diced
- 1 egg
- 1 tablespoon chopped fresh cilantro
- 1 tablespoon crème fraîche (page 9) (sour cream may be substituted)
- 1 teaspoon Dijon mustard
- ¼ teaspoon chipotle powder
- ½ teaspoon salt
- ½ teaspoon pepper
- 1 cup panko (dried bread crumbs may be substituted)
- ½ cup blended oil (page 7)

Preheat the oven to 350°F.

Puree the salmon and half the shrimp in a food processor. Thoroughly mix the salmon mixture, remaining shrimp, vinegar, soy sauce, garlic, bell and jalapeño peppers, onion, egg, cilantro, crème fraîche, mustard, chipotle powder, salt, and pepper in a large bowl.

Form the mixture into 6 cakes for a main course or 12 cakes for a small bite. Coat each cake with panko.

Heat the oil in a sauté pan over medium heat and sauté the cakes until golden brown, 2 to 3 minutes per side.

WINE PAIRING **Sparkling wine or Roussanne**

FOOD FOR THOUGHT *Serve these cakes with a green salad for a light lunch or with mashed potatoes for a hearty dinner. Shrimp and salmon cakes are also wonderful cocktail party food; just prepare the cakes in bite-size portions. Quite a few sauces would complement these cakes, such as Red Pepper Rouille (page 162), Basil Aïoli (page 158), or Citrus Beurre Blanc (page 166).*

Asparagus and Onion Frittata

Serves 6

A frittata is an excellent brunch item to serve to a group of friends because you can make this dish ahead. The best part of this recipe is that you can use whatever vegetables you have in the fridge. In winter try robust vegetables like broccoli and cauliflower florets; and in summer try corn and tomatoes.

- 10 eggs
- ¼ cup half-and-half
- 2 tablespoons unsalted butter
- 1 tablespoon minced garlic
- 1 sweet onion, such as Vidalia or Maui, thinly sliced
- ½ red bell pepper, diced
- ¼ pound asparagus, thinly sliced on the diagonal
- ½ pound mushrooms, sliced
- ¼ pound fresh peas
- salt and pepper
- ½ pound semihard cheese (we like Bell-wether Farms Carmody or Vella Dry Jack), grated (see Sources, page 252)
- 2 tablespoons chopped fresh Italian parsley
- 4 tablespoons chopped fresh tarragon

Preheat the oven to 350°F.

Combine the eggs and half-and-half in a bowl and whisk until smooth. Season with salt and pepper.

Melt the butter in a large ovenproof nonstick sauté pan over medium heat until it begins to brown. Add the garlic, onion, and bell pepper. Sauté the vegetables until they are soft. Remove them from the pan and set aside. Put the asparagus and mushrooms in the sauté pan and cook until just soft. Return the onion mixture to the pan. Add the peas and season with salt and pepper. Add the grated cheese, toss, and heat until the cheese starts to melt slightly. Add the herbs and the egg mixture. Let the mixture cook until the eggs start to set, about 4 to 5 minutes.

Transfer the pan to the oven and cook for about 20 minutes or until the egg is firm in the center of the pan. Let the frittata cool for 20 to 30 minutes. Slide it out of the pan, slice, and serve.

Wine pairing **Marsanne**

Garden Herb Tartlet

MAKES SIX 3½-INCH TARTLETS

At the girl & the fig, one of the most popular items at lunch is our quiche, which is adapted here. Once baked, the tartlet will be light and creamy with an herbal flavor.

Dough

- **2 cups flour**
- **1 teaspoon salt**
- **6 ounces (1½ sticks) unsalted butter, chilled and cut into 1-inch cubes**
- **¼ cup very cold water**

Filling

- **1 tablespoon unsalted butter**
- **1 tablespoon minced garlic**
- **¼ medium onion, diced**
- **2 eggs**
- **1 egg yolk**
- **1½ cups heavy cream**
- **1 tablespoon chopped fresh marjoram**
- **1 tablespoon chopped fresh thyme**
- **1 tablespoon chopped fresh Italian parsley**
- **2 tablespoons flour**
- **1 cup grated Cheddar**

nonstick cooking spray

To make the tartlet shells, combine the flour and salt in a food processor and pulse to incorporate. Add the butter and pulse until it is pea-sized. Add the water and pulse until incorporated. Pour the dough out onto a table and form it into a ball. Wrap the dough with plastic wrap and refrigerate for an hour.

Preheat the oven to 350°F.

Divide the dough into 6 pieces and roll them out to a ⅛-inch thickness. Spray 6 tart molds with nonstick cooking spray and press the dough into the molds. Prick the dough with a fork.

Blind bake (cover the dough with parchment paper and dried beans) for 20 minutes. Remove the parchment and beans and bake for another 5 minutes.

To make the filling, melt the butter in a medium sauté pan over medium heat and sauté the garlic and onion until translucent. Whisk the eggs, egg yolk, cream, and herbs together in a stainless steel bowl. Add the flour, cheese, and onion mixture and mix well. Fill each tartlet shell with ½ cup of the mixture. Bake the tartlets for 10 to 15 minutes or until set.

Wine pairing **Cinsault**

Food for thought *You can add ¼ cup sautéed crispy pancetta or Applewood smoked bacon to the batter for a more savory and substantial tartlet. Serve the tart plain or with a dollop of Roasted Garlic Aïoli (page 159).*

Fig, Prosciutto, and Roquefort Pissaladière

Makes two 12-inch pissaladières

A pissaladière is simply a pizza. In southern France, however, it is not always quite so straightforward. A raw or slightly poached egg often sits on top of a pizza with anchovies, garlic, and the slightest spoonful of fresh tomato. The French eat this as a late-afternoon snack, something to tide them over until a late dinner. This pissaladière is topped with some of our very favorite food combinations but will be delicious with whichever toppings you choose.

Dough

1¼ cups lukewarm water
½ tablespoon dry active yeast
1 teaspoon sugar
1 teaspoon salt
6 teaspoons extra virgin olive oil
3½ cups flour
semolina flour for sprinkling

Toppings

½ cup crumbled Roquefort
6 figs, grilled and cut in sixths
1 cup thinly sliced prosciutto
½ cup Balsamic Onions (page 172)
2 tablespoons extra virgin olive oil
2 tablespoons semolina flour or cornstarch

To make the dough, pour the water in a bowl and sprinkle the yeast and sugar on it. Allow the mixture to begin to foam. In a food processor, work together the salt, 4 teaspoons of the olive oil, and the flour until the dough forms a smooth ball. (It may require more water or flour.)

Coat the inside of a bowl at least twice the size of the dough with the remaining 2 teaspoons olive oil. Place the dough in the bowl, roll it in the oil, and cover with a damp towel. Place the dough in a warm area and allow it to double in size (about 1½ hours). Punch the dough down, let it recover, and let it rest for an additional 30 minutes.

Preheat the oven to 500°F.

Divide the dough into 2 pieces and roll out each piece on a lightly floured surface to a ¼- to ½-inch thickness. Sprinkle a baking sheet with semolina flour and set the dough on top of it. Cover the dough evenly with the topping ingredients, placing the cheese on last. Bake until brown, about 10 minutes. Serve hot or at room temperature.

WINE PAIRING **Fig Royale, Grenache**

FOOD FOR THOUGHT ***For another delicious version of this dish, layer a spoonful of Pistou (page 161) on the dough and top it with your favorite grated hard cheese.***

Chicken Liver Mousse

Makes 4 cups

Our chicken liver mousse is subtle and delicate. Sometimes we serve it in individual ramekins with an assortment of condiments. We also lightly sauce chicken liver mousse quenelles with Tomato Cream Sauce (page 167) and chopped chives for a wonderful small plate. This recipe may yield more mousse than you need, but you can certainly freeze any leftover mousse for a later occasion.

- 4 slices Applewood smoked bacon, chopped
- 2 tablespoons minced shallots
- 2 tablespoons chopped leeks
- 1½ pounds chicken livers, chopped
- 3 eggs
- ½ cup heavy cream
- 3 tablespoons Cognac or brandy
- 2 tablespoons ruby port
- 3 tablespoons chopped fresh Italian parsley
- 1 teaspoon ground ginger
- 2 teaspoons salt
- ½ teaspoon white pepper
- ½ teaspoon nutmeg, freshly grated
- 2 tablespoons flour
- 3 tablespoons unsalted butter, at room temperature
- ½ cup chopped fresh chives
- croutons

Preheat the oven to 375°F.

Place the bacon, shallots, leeks, and livers in a food processor and puree until smooth. Add the eggs, cream, Cognac, port, parsley, ginger, salt, pepper, and nutmeg and blend thoroughly. Slowly work in the flour and continue to puree. Strain the mixture through a fine-mesh sieve to remove large pieces.

Grease an ovenproof dish (large enough to hold 4 cups) with 1 tablespoon of the butter and fill the dish with the liver mixture. Cover the dish with foil, place it in a pan with water that reaches halfway to the top, and put the pan in the oven. Bake for 1 hour 15 minutes or until the center reaches 160°F on an instant-read thermometer. Refrigerate for at least 4 hours or overnight.

In a blender or food processor, whip the remaining 2 tablespoons butter into the mixture. Puree until smooth and adjust the seasoning with salt and pepper. Garnish with chives and croutons.

WINE PAIRING **Grenache**

FOOD FOR THOUGHT ***Serve the mousse in a bowl with an assortment of olives, cornichons, capers, chopped hard-boiled eggs, red onion, and toasted brioche.***

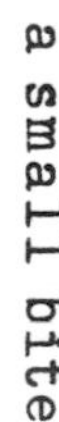
a small bite

charcuterie

Charcuterie may be as simple as a platter of aged sausages with mustard and olives or as complex as a platter of galantines, tourchons, or rillettes. Charcuterie dates back to the fifteenth century, when it was already considered a French culinary art. There are many terrific charcuterie items available in grocery stores today, but if you have some time and patience to make your own, our charcuterie recipes are sure to delight you.

GALANTINE This classic French meat preparation is made with poultry or pork. The meat is boned, stuffed, rolled, and poached in stock until firm. The presentation of a sliced galantine is very beautiful, and often a variety of ingredients is added to emphasize the galantine's appearance. Galantines are generally served cold.

PÂTÉ Traditionally, pâté is a ground meat preparation blended with seasonings, spices, port or wine, dried fruit, and nuts. The texture of pâtés can vary from very smooth and spreadable to coarsely textured, which must be sliced. We regularly change our charcuterie plate and often create new pâté recipes exploring different types of meat and poultry, such as pork, veal, rabbit, chicken liver, and duck.

RILLETTES This rich dish is prepared by slowly poaching meat (typically duck, rabbit, or pork) in seasoned fat until tender and then whipping it with a small amount of butter or other fat. The rillette is served in small pots or ramekins as a cold spread. We add vegetables and herbs to our rillettes for an earthy flavor.

A **TERRINE** is technically a pâté cooked and served in its mold or container (a pâté has been removed from its container).

John's love of pork products has inspired him to create our wonderful charcuterie dishes. He is very experimental and even prepares his own prosciutto, not only with a leg of pork but with duck breasts as well.

These are some of the charcuterie combinations served at the girl & the fig:

Chicken liver mousse, roasted tomato sauce, scallions, croutons

Dried cherry and pistachio pork terrine, prosciutto di Parma, fig-cranberry compote, spiced nuts, croutons

Pork rillette, prosciutto-wrapped stuffed pork tenderloin, apricot-fig chutney with sage, Dijon mustard, caperberries, croutons

Accompaniments to Charcuterie

Apricot-fig chutney
Fig balsamic reduction
Dijon mustard or whole-grain mustard
Cranberry relish
Orange marmalade
Capers or caperberries
Olive tapenade
Cornichons
Fresh figs
Dried apricots
Zante grapes
Bosc pears
Fuji apples
Hazelnut toasts
Olive bread
Brioche croutons
Sea salt
Freshly cracked pepper

Duck and Mushroom Rillettes

Makes 2½ cups

A rillette is another one of our favored charcuterie items. It is quite simple to prepare and uses leftover ingredients. Duck, rabbit, or pork can easily become a rillette by being poached in fat (similar to the confit technique, page 140) and then whipped with a small amount of the fat or butter. Rillettes are generally served in small ramekins, but a decorative bowl with complementary garnishes would work just as well.

2 tablespoons unsalted butter
½ cup cremini mushrooms, chopped
2 tablespoons minced shallots
½ tablespoon minced garlic
1 tablespoon chopped fresh tarragon
1 tablespoon chopped fresh Italian parsley
4 confited duck legs (see page 140), shredded
salt and white pepper
3 tablespoons crème fraîche (page 9) (sour cream may be substituted)

Melt the butter in a sauté pan. Add the mushrooms and shallots and cook gently until tender, about 5 minutes. Add the garlic, tarragon, parsley, and shredded duck and break up with a wooden spoon (the mixture will look stringy). Season with salt and pepper. Remove from the heat and add the crème fraîche. Blend the mixture with a wooden spoon until the ingredients are incorporated.

Fill 3-ounce ramekins with the mixture and refrigerate for at least 30 minutes before serving.

Wine pairing **Lillet blanc**

Food for thought *Serve the rillettes with toasted croutons, whole-grain mustard, and cornichons. If you are making the duck confit (page 140) or Duck Cassoulet (page 142), this is a great recipe to make with the leftover duck. (It is not practical to prepare duck confit just for this dish.)*

Foie Gras Tourchon with Dried Fig Compote

MAKES ONE 3 BY 12-INCH TOURCHON

Every year we serve this tourchon on Valentine's Day and New Year's Eve. If you find foie gras irresistible and want to treat yourself to a gourmet delight, make the effort to prepare this tourchon. ("Tourchon" refers to shaping the charcuterie into a cylinder. Other ingredients may be used to create a tourchon as well.) This is a decadent dish for very special occasions. It is a time-consuming recipe requiring a bit of patience, but you will find that it is well worth the effort.

- 1 foie gras, grade B (not perfect, but very good for this recipe)
- 8 cups milk
- 3 teaspoons salt
- 1 teaspoon white pepper
- 3 quarts chicken stock (page 11)
- 1 teaspoon black peppercorns
- bouquet garni (3 thyme sprigs, 3 Italian parsley sprigs, 1 bay leaf)
- 1 onion, chopped
- 1 carrot, peeled and chopped
- 1 celery stalk, chopped
- Dried Fig Compote (recipe follows)

Place the foie gras in a bowl, cover with the milk, and soak for 48 hours.

Remove the foie gras from the milk and pat dry with a towel. Allow the foie gras to reach room temperature. Remove the outside membrane and veins from the foie gras. At this point the foie gras will take on a claylike consistency, allowing you to reshape it after removing the veins and blemishes. Once you have removed as many veins and blemishes as possible, reshape the liver as closely as possible to its original form. Sprinkle the liver evenly with the salt and pepper and allow it to sit for an additional 8 hours in the refrigerator.

Remove the liver from the refrigerator and allow it to come to room temperature. Using your hands, shape the liver into a 3-inch cylinder. Using cheesecloth, wrap the liver as tightly as possible into an evenly shaped cylinder. (This is a two-person job, with one person holding the cheesecloth and the other rolling.) The tourchon should be rolled so tight that liver oozes slightly through the cloth.

Once the foie gras has been rolled and tied, bring the stock to a boil with the peppercorns, bouquet garni, onion, carrot, and celery.

Set up an ice-water bath large enough to hold the tourchon completely submerged.

Place the tourchon in the hot stock and poach for 90 seconds. Immediately remove to the water bath and allow to chill. (Save the stock for soup or another recipe.)

Once the tourchon has chilled, retie the ends to ensure that the tourchon is once again wrapped as tightly as possible. Find a place in your refrigerator to hang the tourchon and let it hang for at least 24 hours.

Unwrap the tourchon and cut into slices of the desired thickness.

Dried Fig Compote

MAKES 2½ CUPS

3 tablespoons minced shallots
¼ cup olive oil
2 cups dried figs, quartered
¼ cup mustard seeds
½ cup sugar
1 cup fig balsamic vinegar (balsamic vinegar may be substituted)
2 tablespoons whole-grain mustard
pepper

Sauté the shallots in the olive oil in a medium saucepan over medium-high heat until translucent. Add the figs, mustard seeds, sugar, vinegar, mustard, and pepper. Reduce the heat and simmer until the figs are soft and the compote has thickened to the consistency of fruit preserves.

WINE PAIRING **Sparkling wine**

FOOD FOR THOUGHT ***In addition to the fig compote, the following accompaniments are lovely with the foie gras tourchon: Balsamic Shallots (page 172), Pickled Figs (page 62), coarse sea salt, and toasted brioche.***

Pork and Dried Cherry Pâté

MAKES 1 LARGE PÂTÉ (ABOUT 3½ POUNDS)

The dried cherries add a bit of sweetness and the hazelnuts add another layer of texture to this pork pâté. We change our charcuterie plate regularly and often create new pâtés from our base recipes. The accompaniments also change, which provides varying flavors and textures.

2 teaspoons crushed red pepper
2 bay leaves
1 teaspoon coriander seeds, toasted
2 teaspoons anise seed, toasted
1 clove
2 teaspoons dried thyme
2 teaspoons minced garlic
2½ pounds ground pork butt (medium grind)
½ pound ground pork fatback (medium grind)
2 tablespoons salt
1 teaspoon pepper
¼ cup sugar
1 egg
1 cup dried cherries
1 cup hazelnuts, toasted

Grind the red pepper, bay leaves, coriander, anise, clove, and thyme in a spice or coffee grinder. Mix in the garlic and set aside. Put the ground pork butt and fatback, spice mix, salt, pepper, and sugar in a large bowl and combine thoroughly. Allow the mixture to marinate for at least 24 hours.

Preheat the oven to 350°F.

Remove the meat mixture from the refrigerator and allow it to come to room temperature. Add the egg, dried cherries, and hazelnuts and mix to incorporate the flavors. Cook a small piece of the mixture in a pan to taste the seasoning; adjust as needed.

Place the mixture in a pâté mold. Place the mold in a pan, add water that reaches halfway to the top of the pan, and cover with foil. Bake the pâté in the pan for about 1½ hours or until the center reaches 160°F on an instant-read thermometer. Remove the pâté from the oven and let cool before serving.

WINE PAIRING **Grenache**

FOOD FOR THOUGHT *Serve this recipe with a drizzle of Balsamic Reduction (page 91) or Balsamic Shallots (page 172). I like the way the sharpness of the balsamic flavor heightens the flavors of the pork and contrasts with the flavors of the cherries. For a simpler approach, serve the pâté with whole-grain or Dijon mustard, olives, caperberries, toast, and dried apricots.*

Rabbit and Hazelnut Pâté with Pickled Figs

Makes 1 quart (2¼ pounds)

This is one of our most popular charcuterie recipes. We often feature it in spring, when we offer our braised Sonoma rabbit. Charcuterie items are not difficult to prepare—they are just time-consuming and sometimes frustrating for chefs who want to eat their creations right away! You can freeze any leftover pâté to enjoy at a later date.

- 3 tablespoons minced shallots
- 1 tablespoon herbes de Provence
- 1 teaspoon coriander
- ½ teaspoon crushed red pepper
- 4 bay leaves
- 1 rabbit, boned by the butcher and cubed, loins sliced in half
- 1 pound pork sausage
- 1 egg
- 2 tablespoons blended oil (page 7)
- 2 tablespoons gin
- salt and pepper
- ½ cup hazelnuts, toasted and skinned
- 4 slices bacon
- Pickled Figs (recipe follows)

Combine the shallots, spices, and bay leaves in a food processor and process for 15 seconds. Add the cubed rabbit and process until the mixture is smooth, 1 to 2 minutes. Remove the mixture from the processor and place it in a large bowl. Add the sausage, egg, oil, and gin. Season with salt and pepper. Using your hands, thoroughly blend the ingredients. Wrap the mixture in plastic wrap and allow it to sit in the refrigerator overnight.

Preheat the oven to 350°F.

Fill a terrine halfway with the pâté. Run 2 strips of the rabbit loin down the center of the terrine, leaving a ½-inch gap between them. Place the hazelnuts in the middle of the 2 strips of loin. Fill the terrine with the remaining mixture and cover with the bacon; cover the terrine with foil. Place the terrine in a larger pan and fill the pan with water that reaches halfway to the top. Bake the pâté in the pan for about an hour or until the center of the terrine reaches 160°F on an instant-read thermometer. Place the pâté in the refrigerator and weight down the top with cans or bags of beans. Allow to cool overnight. Serve at room temperature.

Pickled Figs

YIELD 1½ CUPS

- 1 vanilla bean
- ½ cup Figoun (see Sources, page 254) (cassis may be substituted)
- 1 cup Champagne vinegar
- ¾ cup sugar
- ½ cup framboise
- 1 kaffir lime leaf (zest of 2 limes may be substituted)
- 2 tablespoons honey
- ½ teaspoon sea salt
- 1 teaspoon white pepper
- 15 fresh figs, stems removed

Split the vanilla bean in half and put into 1 cup water with the Figoun, vinegar, sugar, framboise, lime leaf, honey, salt, and pepper in a large saucepan. Bring the liquid to a boil. Add the figs, reduce to a simmer, and cook for about 7 minutes, then remove from the heat. Allow the figs to cool in the liquid before removing them.

The liquid can be used to pickle other fruit, like apricots and plums. The figs will keep in the refrigerator for 7 days.

WINE PAIRING Cinsault or Grenache

FOOD FOR THOUGHT *Figoun is a French fig liqueur not easily found. Many liqueurs can be substituted. Cassis gives a currant flavor, Chambord and framboise lend a raspberry flavor, and Calvados lends an apple flavor.*

Crispy Sweetbreads

Serves 6

Every year around late fall and early winter, John starts to think about sweetbreads. Every year we have the same conversation about how delicious they are but how hardly anyone ever orders them. Inevitably, we put them on the menu every year to please guests who can't find them elsewhere.

1½ pounds sweetbreads
6 cups chicken stock (page 11)
1 large onion, roughly chopped
1 celery stalk, roughly chopped
½ carrot, peeled and roughly chopped
1 bay leaf
2 teaspoons black peppercorns
4 fresh thyme sprigs
4 fresh Italian parsley sprigs
½ cup semolina flour
2 teaspoons salt
½ teaspoon pepper
½ cup blended oil (page 7)

Soak the sweetbreads in water overnight.

In a stockpot, bring the chicken stock to a simmer. Blanch the sweetbreads in the simmering stock with the onion, celery, carrot, bay leaf, peppercorns, thyme, and parsley for 8 to 10 minutes until just cooked through (they should be tender and semifirm). Remove the sweetbreads from the stock, shock them in ice water, and drain. Press overnight by putting the sweetbreads in a pan, covering them, and weighting them with a heavy object.

Remove the membrane and sinewy parts from the sweetbreads and slice the sweetbreads into 1-inch pieces.

Mix the semolina flour with the salt and pepper. Dredge the sweetbreads in the flour mixture and shake off the excess flour. Heat the oil in a large skillet to 350°F. (The sweetbreads must be at least half covered by the oil.) Pan-fry the sweetbreads in small batches until golden brown all over, about 4–5 minutes. Drain on paper towels and serve hot.

Wine pairing **Grenache Rosé or Syrah**

Food for thought *Serve the sweetbreads in a large bowl over Wilted Greens (page 177) with shaved Parmesan or with Wild Mushroom Ragout (page 182).*

The chefs at the girl & the fig love to prepare soup. They choose recipes according to what is fresh, seasonal, and, most of all, what inspires them. The preparation of soup requires a slower pace than the rapid execution of dishes made to order. This more relaxed pace of preparation gives the chefs the time to organize their day and mentally prepare themselves for the dinner service ahead. Even though many of our soup recipes are quite easy, they shouldn't be rushed. Slow cooking allows the ingredients to meld and brings out the best flavors. The intensity of the vegetable flavors changes during the season, so try to choose vegetables at their peak ripeness.

from the garden to the stockpot

Heirloom Tomato Gazpacho
Fire-Roasted Eggplant Soup
Carrot-Ginger Soup
Asparagus and English Pea Soup with Pistachio Butter
Spring Vidalia Onion and Mushroom Soup with Morel Croutons
Butternut Squash Soup with Apple Compote
Potted Chicken and Corn Soup
Provençal Seafood Stew
Crab and Mushroom Chowder
Cauliflower Gruyère Soup
Potato Leek Soup
White Bean and Duck Confit Soup

Heirloom Tomato Gazpacho

Serves 6

There are many variations of gazpacho, but what I like about ours is the distinct flavor and texture of the tomatoes. If you start out with ripe, sweet-smelling tomatoes, your gazpacho will be lovely.

In keeping with our concept of "country food with a French passion," the addition of fennel, tarragon, balsamic vinegar, and a splash of Pernod gives this gazpacho a Provençal flavor.

- 3 pounds heirloom tomatoes
- 1 red bell pepper, seeded and diced
- 1 cup diced fennel
- 1 cucumber, peeled and chopped
- 1 red onion, chopped
- ¼ cup sherry vinegar
- 1 tablespoon balsamic vinegar
- ¼ cup extra virgin olive oil
- ¼ cup Pernod
- ½ tablespoon minced garlic
- ¼ cup chopped fresh Italian parsley
- 2 tablespoons chopped fresh thyme
- ¼ cup chopped fresh tarragon
- sea salt and pepper

Using a knife, score the bottoms of the tomatoes with an X. In a pot of boiling water, blanch the tomatoes for 30 seconds to loosen the skins. Plunge the tomatoes in ice water and drain. Peel the skins from the tomatoes and cut them in half. Working over a bowl, gently squeeze the tomato halves to release the seeds and juice. Strain the tomato juice, pressing on the solids to extract as much juice as possible. Discard the seeds and chop the tomatoes.

Transfer the chopped tomatoes and the juice to a large glass bowl. Add the bell pepper, fennel, cucumber, red onion, both vinegars, olive oil, Pernod, garlic, and herbs and let stand at room temperature for an hour.

Puree half the gazpacho mixture in a blender until smooth. Add the puree to the remaining gazpacho and mix well. Season with salt and pepper. Chill the soup for at least 2 hours and up to a day. Serve cold.

Wine pairing **Roussanne**

heirloom tomatoes

Heirloom tomatoes have been the rage for at least the past six years. Many farmers are dedicated to rediscovering the fruits and vegetables first grown and written about in the 1800s, now called heirloom varieties. Each year there are more and more heirloom selections to choose from. These products are exciting from a taste standpoint, but the array of varieties gives a boost to the cook's imagination as well. Our main produce supplier, Greenleaf Produce, in San Francisco, has an incredible network of tomato farmers who supply us with a wide range of tomatoes. Tomato season can never start early enough for us!

BRANDYWINE are large reddish-pink tomatoes with a solid sweet flesh. These tomatoes date back to 1885 in Amish country and can grow as large as 1½ pounds.

CHEROKEE PURPLE weigh ½ to ¾ pound and are dusty rose colored. These are very sweet, low in acid, and have a rich flavor.

EARLY GIRL tomatoes are the first tomatoes of the season. They are small, vine-ripened, and very versatile.

GOLDEN QUEEN were the first heirloom tomatoes, introduced in 1882. These mild, sweet tomatoes with a vivid yellow color average ½ to ¾ pound in size. They are very meaty, with relatively few seeds.

GREEN ZEBRA is a very unusual tomato variety, which we use every summer in our salads. They are bright green with light green stripes, weigh in at ½ pound, and have a delicious, sweet, and zingy flavor with high acidity.

TANGERINE tomatoes are bright yellow-orange beefsteaks. They are meaty in texture and have a complex sweet flavor.

YELLOW PEARS are pear-shaped, bite-size tomatoes with yellow skin and flesh that date back to the late 1800s. They grow in clusters and have an excellent sweet flavor. These tomatoes brighten up salads and pastas.

Fire-Roasted Eggplant Soup

Serves 6

Michael, our sous chef, created this recipe in the original girl & the fig kitchen for an article on eggplants a few years ago. I love the way the grill looks with the purple-skinned eggplants lined up. This is a recipe you can start on your outdoor grill over a charcoal fire and finish over the stove. The balsamic vinegar helps caramelize the eggplant skins and gives this soup a unique flavor.

2 pounds Japanese eggplant, trimmed and cut lengthwise
3 tablespoons blended oil (page 7)
1 tablespoon balsamic vinegar
salt and pepper
1 tablespoon unsalted butter
2 medium onions, sliced thin
1 quart chicken stock (page 11)
2 tablespoons lemon juice
2 tablespoons Dijon mustard
¼ cup crème fraîche
¼ cup Roasted Red Peppers (page 9), thinly sliced

Toss the eggplant gently with 2 tablespoons of the oil, the balsamic vinegar, salt, and pepper in a stainless steel bowl. Char the eggplant on a grill, turning to cook evenly. Set the eggplant aside.

Heat the remaining tablespoon of oil and the butter over medium heat in a large saucepan and sauté the onions until translucent. Chop the grilled eggplant and add to the sauteéd onions. Cover with the chicken stock. Bring to a boil and cover. Reduce the heat and simmer for 30 minutes.

Puree the soup mixture in a blender and add the lemon juice and Dijon mustard. Adjust the seasoning with salt and pepper. Ladle the soup into bowls and garnish with crème fraîche and roasted pepper slices.

Wine pairing **Cinsault**

Carrot-Ginger Soup

Serves 6

Carrots scream spring! Even though there is an ample supply of carrots all year round, carrot soup in spring celebrates the beginning of the season. Baby carrots in all colors and shapes fill the stalls at the Tuesday night farmer's market in Sonoma. We have been particularly fond of the maroon carrots—these colorful roots add a zip of color to the plate.

In this recipe we have added lime juice to balance the sugar of the carrots with some acidity, and the ginger gives the soup another layer of flavor.

2 tablespoons unsalted butter
1 medium onion, chopped
2 leeks, whites only, chopped
½ fennel bulb, diced
1 tablespoon minced fresh ginger
6 cups chicken stock (page 11)
3 pounds carrots, peeled and sliced
½ cup heavy cream
3 tablespoons lime juice
salt and pepper
crème fraîche (page 9)

Melt the butter in a large heavy saucepan over medium-high heat. Add the onion, leeks, fennel, and ginger and sauté until the vegetables are translucent, 5 to 7 minutes. Add the chicken stock and carrots. Cover and simmer until the carrots are tender, about 35 minutes.

Working in batches, puree the mixture in a blender. Blend in the cream and lime juice. Strain and season to taste. Thin the soup with about ¾ cup warm water if necessary. Drizzle crème fraîche on the soup as a garnish.

Wine pairing **Marsanne**

oak hill farm

Ted Bucklin, Glen Ellen, California

When we first opened the restaurant in Glen Ellen, a man came in wearing high rubber boots. His hands were caked with dirt, his face soaked with sweat. In his arms were a bundle of freshly picked flowers and a box of tomatoes that I traded for a cold beer. That was my warm welcome to the neighborhood and how I met Ted Bucklin. He invited me up to his farm and offered to plant anything we needed for our kitchen.

Since that day, Oak Hill Farm has been my favorite place to shop for flowers and vegetables. The extensive farm offers beautiful herbs, flowers, onions, garlic, apples, pears, peppers, heirloom tomatoes, greens, potatoes, summer and winter squash, turnips, carrots, and a fig tree, of course. Located in an old barn between the orchards and the farm, the farm store is not overloaded with produce. They harvest every day and offer only the best of what the garden produced that day. The store itself is a fabulous sensory experience. The brilliant colors, smells, and flavors are a treat every time. The Oak Hill Farm staff also produces the most beautiful wreaths with dried flowers from their gardens, which we display in the restaurants every year at holiday time.

Asparagus and English Pea Soup with Pistachio Butter

Serves 6

Asparagus soup is one of the most popular soups we serve. The delicate spring flavors of fresh asparagus and English peas are a nice combination, while the pistachio butter adds texture and a nutty flavor to this beautiful soup.

- 1½ pounds asparagus, 12 tips reserved separately, ends trimmed, stalks chopped
- 1⅓ cups shelled English peas
- 3 tablespoons blended oil (page 7)
- 1 medium onion, chopped
- 2 teaspoons minced garlic
- 1 small fennel bulb, chopped
- 1 celery stalk, chopped
- ½ medium potato, peeled and chopped
- 1 tablespoon chopped fresh Italian parsley
- ½ tablespoon salt
- 3 tablespoons unsalted butter, room temperature
- 1 tablespoon lemon juice
- salt and pepper
- Pistachio Butter (recipe follows)

In a pot of boiling water, blanch the asparagus tips and ⅓ cup of the peas. Set aside.

In a large saucepan, heat the oil over medium heat and sauté the onion, garlic, fennel, and celery until soft. Add the asparagus stalks and cook until soft, about 5 minutes. Add the potato, the remaining 1 cup peas, and the parsley. Season with the salt. Add 4 cups water and bring the mixture to a boil. Simmer for 30 minutes and then turn off the heat. Let the mixture cool slightly.

In batches, puree the vegetables in a blender with the butter and lemon juice until smooth. Adjust the seasoning with salt and pepper. Return the soup to the heat. Serve warm, garnished with Pistachio Butter.

Pistachio Butter

MAKES 1¼ CUPS

- ½ cup toasted pistachio nuts
- 1 tablespoon minced shallots
- ¼ pound (1 stick) unsalted butter, at room temperature
- 1 tablespoon chopped fresh Italian parsley
- ½ tablespoon chopped fresh thyme
- 1 tablespoon orange juice
- 2 teaspoons salt
- ½ teaspoon white pepper

Combine all the ingredients in a food processor and puree until medium smooth. Spoon a generous dollop of butter into each serving of soup.

WINE PAIRING Roussanne

Spring Vidalia Onion and Mushroom Soup with Morel Croutons

SERVES 6

Though this soup has three steps and is a bit time-consuming to prepare, it really is a very simple, elegant soup that celebrates springtime in the wine country. Vidalia onions give the soup a sweet flavor, and the rustic flavor of the mushrooms will lighten up with the rich cream. If morels are available, they will be just perfect for the croutons. Otherwise substitute shiitake, cremini, chanterelle, or hedgehog mushrooms.

Mushroom stock

- **½ ounce dried morel mushrooms**
- **1 cup diced onion**
- **1 tablespoon minced garlic**
- **1 tablespoon olive oil**
- **9 cups chicken stock (page 11)**

Soup

- **4 tablespoons (½ stick) unsalted butter**
- **8 cups thinly sliced Vidalia onions (any type of sweet onion may be substituted)**
- **2 cups fresh mushrooms, cleaned and cut in half**
- **salt and pepper**
- **1 tablespoon fresh thyme**
- **½ cup white wine**
- **½ cup heavy cream**

Morel croutons

- **4 tablespoons (½ stick) unsalted butter, at room temperature**
- **2 teaspoons minced shallots**
- **¼ cup grated hard cheese, such as Parmesan or aged Cheddar**
- **1 tablespoon dry vermouth**
- **salt and pepper**
- **12 slices French baguette, toasted**

Rehydrate the morels with a cup of boiling water and let sit for 15 minutes.

Sauté the onion and garlic in the olive oil in a large saucepan. Add the morels, morel liquid, and chicken stock.

Bring to a boil and then reduce the heat to a simmer for 15 minutes. Let cool. Let sit in the refrigerator for at least 4 hours or overnight to let the flavors meld. Strain and reserve the mushrooms for the croutons.

In a heavy-bottomed saucepan, melt the butter over medium heat. Cook the onions and mushrooms until golden brown and caramelized, 5 to 6 minutes. Season with salt and pepper. Add the thyme and deglaze the pan with the white wine. Add 8 cups of the mushroom stock and the heavy cream and simmer for about 20 minutes. Adjust the seasoning.

To make the croutons, combine the butter, shallots, cheese, dry vermouth, and 3 tablespoons of the reserved morels in the food processor. Puree to a creamy paste. Season with salt and pepper and spread liberally on toasted bread slices. To serve, place 2 slices on each bowl of soup.

WINE PAIRING Roussanne

Butternut Squash Soup with Apple Compote

Serves 6

This is one of my favorite winter soups. Butternut squash is loaded with flavor, and when roasted, those flavors deepen. The curry powder gives the soup a surprise taste and the apple compote adds a sweet essence as well as texture.

3 pounds butternut squash, cut lengthwise and seeded
¼ cup blended oil (page 7)
1 tablespoon light brown sugar
salt and pepper
½ tablespoon minced garlic
1 medium onion, chopped
1 Fuji apple, peeled, cored, and chopped
6 tablespoons unsalted butter, chilled
3 cups chicken stock (page 11)
pinch of curry powder
1 cup heavy cream
1 tablespoon lemon juice
Apple Compote (recipe follows)

Preheat the oven to 400°F.

Place the squash cut side up in an ovenproof pan. Drizzle the squash with the oil and brown sugar and season with salt and pepper. Bake until the squash is tender and golden brown, about 45 minutes.

In a large saucepan, sauté the garlic, onion, and apple in 2 tablespoons of the butter until the mixture is translucent. Using a large spoon, scrape the squash into the pan (discard the squash peel).

Add the chicken stock and curry powder and simmer for 10 minutes. Mix in the cream and lemon juice. Pour the mixture into a food processor or blender and puree until smooth. Whisk the remaining 4 tablespoons chilled butter into the pureed soup and stir the soup over medium heat until heated through. Season to taste with salt and pepper. Serve with the Apple Compote.

Apple Compote

Makes 2 cups

2 Fuji apples, cored, peeled, and diced
¼ cup plus 2 tablespoons lime juice
¼ cup quartered dried apricots
¼ cup dried cherries
½ cup simple syrup (page 8)
1 cinnamon stick
pinch of nutmeg, freshly grated
1 teaspoon mustard seeds

Toss the apple with the 2 tablespoons lime juice in a bowl. Set aside.

Simmer the apricots, cherries, syrup, ½ cup water, the ¼ cup lime juice, the cinnamon stick, nutmeg, and mustard seeds in a saucepan for 10 minutes. Add the apples and simmer for an additional 5 minutes. Remove the pot from the heat.

Garnish the Butternut Squash Soup with a heaping tablespoon of compote.

Wine pairing **Marsanne**

Food for thought ***You can substitute crumbled blue cheese for the Apple Compote for a richer, more robust flavor. Leftover Apple Compote can accompany charcuterie or cheese plates.***

Potted Chicken and Corn Soup

SERVES 6

This is a relatively simple soup to prepare, and is somewhat similar to my mom's cure-all for the common cold. Our sous chef Michael's sautéed corn adds a bit of sweetness to this chicken soup. The chicken and stock can be prepared a day ahead.

1 chicken (about 3 pounds)
3 quarts chicken stock (page 11)
¼ pound pancetta, diced
1 tablespoon blended oil (page 7)
½ cup diced onion
½ cup diced peeled carrot
¼ cup diced fennel
¼ cup diced red bell pepper
salt and pepper
1 teaspoon minced garlic
1 tablespoon chopped fresh thyme
1 cup corn kernels (from about 1 ear fresh corn)
1 cup peeled, diced Yukon Gold potato
1 tablespoon chopped fresh Italian parsley
3 tablespoons chopped fennel fronds

Cook the whole chicken in a large saucepan in the chicken stock over medium heat for about 1¼ hours (the chicken meat should be falling off the bones). Remove the chicken from the stock and cool. Strain the stock and reduce it to 1½ quarts (6 cups). Skim off any fat. Pour the stock into a container and reserve.

When the chicken has cooled enough to work with, pick the meat off the bones and break it up into bite-size pieces. Set the meat aside and discard the carcass.

In the saucepan, sauté the pancetta in the oil over medium heat until crispy. Add the onion, carrot, fennel, and bell pepper and cook until just soft. Season with salt and pepper. Add the garlic, thyme, and corn and sauté for another minute. Add the reserved stock, chicken meat, and potato and cook until the potato softens, about 15 minutes. Add the parsley and fennel tops and adjust the seasoning.

WINE PAIRING Viognier

Provençal Seafood Stew

Serves 6

Our stew begins with our rich lobster stock made from roasted lobster shells. It is embellished with fresh vegetables, shellfish, and fish. The richness of the lobster stock and the freshness of the vegetables are a delicious combination.

2 leeks, julienned
1 onion, julienned
2 celery stalks, julienned
1 fennel bulb, julienned
3 tablespoons blended oil (page 7)
3 garlic cloves, crushed
salt and pepper
6 cups lobster stock (page 12)
3 tomatoes, peeled and roughly chopped
12 sea scallops
¾ pound salmon fillet, cut into 1-inch cubes
18 mussels
18 clams
½ pound rock shrimp
½ cup white wine
3 tablespoons Pernod
3 tablespoons unsalted butter

Sauté the leeks, onion, celery, and fennel in 1 tablespoon of the oil in a large saucepan over medium heat until the vegetables are translucent. Add the garlic and season with salt and pepper. Sauté until the mixture begins to brown. Add the stock and tomatoes and bring to a boil. Lower the heat and simmer for 15 minutes.

In another large saucepan heat the remaining 2 tablespoons of the oil and sear the scallops and salmon. Add the mussels, clams, and shrimp and deglaze with the white wine and Pernod. Add the stock, bring it to a boil, and cook until the clams and mussels open, 5 to 6 minutes. Add the butter and adjust the seasoning.

Wine pairing **Marsanne**

Food for thought *Serve with toasted baguette and a drizzle of Roasted Garlic Aïoli (page 159).*

Crab and Mushroom Chowder

Serves 6

When Dungeness crab is in season, it tastes good in just about everything. My favorite way to eat it is chilled, on its own, with no sauce. These crabs are rich in flavor and are very meaty. Buy several crabs and use some for this soup recipe, some for the Dungeness Crab Cakes (page 42), and use the claw meat in an omelet or in the Garden Herb Tartlet (page 47). Buy your crabs as fresh as possible, and have your fishmonger crack and clean them for you.

2 tablespoons unsalted butter
1 medium onion, chopped
1 celery stalk, chopped
1 carrot, peeled and chopped
2 teaspoons minced garlic
½ large red bell pepper, chopped
¼ cup chopped fennel
¼ pound Chanterelle mushrooms, chopped into medium-size pieces (shiitakes or cremini may be substituted)
1 tablespoon chopped fresh thyme
2 teaspoons chopped fresh marjoram
1 bay leaf
¼ cup white wine
small pinch of saffron threads
5 cups chicken stock (page 11) or 2 cups lobster (page 12) plus 3 cups chicken stock
1 russet potato, peeled and diced
1 cup diced canned stewed tomatoes, juice reserved
¾ pound Dungeness crabmeat
salt and pepper

Melt the butter in a large saucepan over medium heat. Add the onion, celery, carrot, and garlic and sauté until the vegetables are soft. Add the bell pepper and fennel and continue to sauté for a few more minutes. Add the mushrooms, thyme, marjoram, and bay leaf and cook until the mushrooms are soft and tender. Deglaze the pan with the white wine and add the saffron threads. Add the chicken stock, potatoes, and tomatoes. Cook until the potatoes are soft, about 15 minutes. Gently incorporate the crabmeat. Don't overstir. Season with salt and pepper as needed.

WINE PAIRING **Viognier**

FOOD FOR THOUGHT ***If Chanterelle mushrooms are not available, substitute shiitake or cremini mushrooms. If you have lobster stock, you can use 2 cups lobster stock and 3 cups chicken stock.***

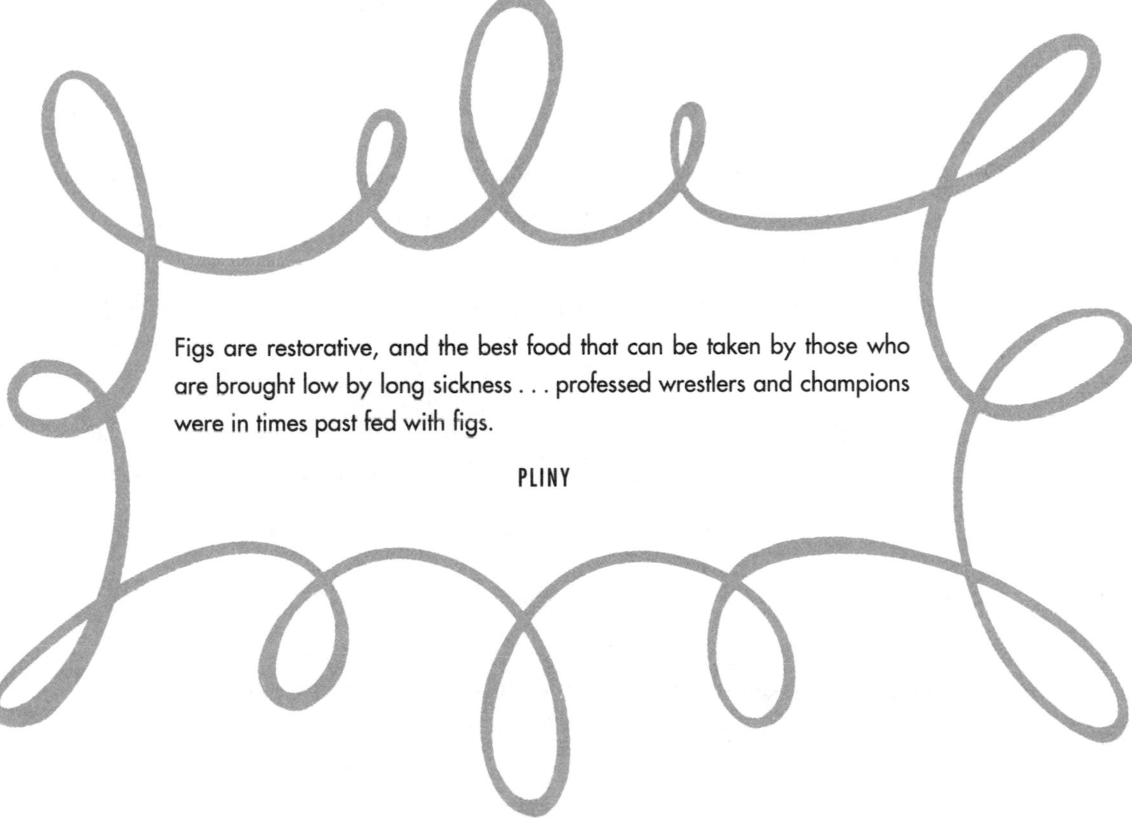

Figs are restorative, and the best food that can be taken by those who are brought low by long sickness . . . professed wrestlers and champions were in times past fed with figs.

PLINY

Cauliflower Gruyère Soup

Serves 6

Cauliflower is an underrated vegetable. Simply roasted with olive oil, cauliflower is a sophisticated and delicious side dish, but its flavor is even more delicious in a soup. Our version of cauliflower soup is enhanced by tangy Gruyère cheese.

3 tablespoons unsalted butter
1 onion, thinly sliced
1 head cauliflower, broken into small florets
salt and white pepper
½ tablespoon minced garlic
1 quart chicken stock (page 11)
bouquet garni (3 Italian parsley sprigs, 1 tarragon sprig, 3 thyme sprigs, 1 bay leaf)
¼ pound grated Gruyère
½ cup heavy cream
¼ cup chopped chives

Melt 2 tablespoons of the butter in a large saucepan and cook the onion slowly until soft and translucent but not browned. Add the cauliflower, season lightly with salt and pepper, and cook over low heat for another 10 minutes, stirring occasionally so the mixture does not brown. Add the remaining 1 tablespoon butter. Add the garlic and cook for 5 more minutes, allowing the mixture to brown slightly. Add the stock and bouquet garni and bring the mixture to a boil. Once the soup has come to a rolling boil reduce to a simmer, cover, and cook for 25 to 30 minutes. Remove the bouquet garni.

Using a blender, puree the soup in batches, slowly adding the Gruyère. Add up to about ½ cup of the cream to obtain the desired thickness. Adjust the seasoning and garnish with the chives.

Wine pairing **Viognier**

Note: If the soup is too thick, you may use either heavy cream or water to thin it out.

Potato Leek Soup

Serves 6

Here, truffle oil and fennel revitalize the classic vichyssoise recipe. This is a quick soup that will become a staple in your kitchen. The velvety texture and creamy richness is a crowd pleaser every time.

- 3 leeks, whites only, diced
- 1 fennel bulb, diced
- 5 tablespoons unsalted butter, chilled
- 4 cups chicken stock (page 11)
- 1½ pounds russet potatoes, peeled and chopped into 1-inch pieces
- 2 tablespoons chopped fresh thyme
- 2 tablespoons chopped fresh tarragon
- 2 tablespoons chopped fresh Italian parsley
- salt and white pepper
- 2 cups milk
- ½ cup heavy cream
- 2 tablespoons lemon juice
- truffle oil

Sauté the leeks and fennel in a large saucepan over high heat with 3 tablespoons of the butter until translucent. Add the chicken stock, potatoes, and herbs. Season with salt and pepper. Cover and cook over medium heat for about 30 minutes. Blend the mixture in a blender with the milk, cream, lemon juice, and the remaining 2 tablespoons butter. Strain. Drizzle each serving with truffle oil before serving.

Wine pairing Viognier

White Bean and Duck Confit Soup

Serves 6

John created this soup so that more of our guests would experience the wonderful rich flavors of duck confit. With a simple green salad, this hearty soup can be served as a meal. We use cannellini beans, but Great White Northern beans or Gigante beans are other options.

1 cup dried cannellini beans, soaked overnight
1 bay leaf
¼ pound prosciutto, julienned
½ cup diced onion
3 tablespoons minced garlic
2 tablespoons blended oil (page 7)
3 carrots, peeled and sliced into ½-inch rounds
3 leeks, sliced into ½-inch rounds
¼ head savoy cabbage, chopped
2 tablespoons chopped fresh thyme
1 tablespoon chopped fresh sage
salt and pepper
2½ quarts chicken stock (page 11)
1 large Yukon Gold potato, peeled and cut into 1-inch cubes
2 confited duck legs, meat only (dark meat from a roasted chicken may be substituted)

In a large pot, cover the beans and bay leaf with water and simmer for 40 minutes. Drain and set aside.

In a separate large saucepan, sauté the prosciutto, onion, and garlic in the oil over medium heat until the garlic begins to brown. Add the carrots, leeks, cabbage, and herbs and sauté for an additional 10 minutes over low heat. Stir occasionally to mix the ingredients, making sure not to burn the bottom of the pan; add more oil if needed. Season with salt and pepper. Cover the mixture with the chicken stock and bring to a boil. Add the potato, duck confit, and beans and simmer until the beans and potatoes are soft. Adjust the seasoning.

Wine pairing **Cinsault**

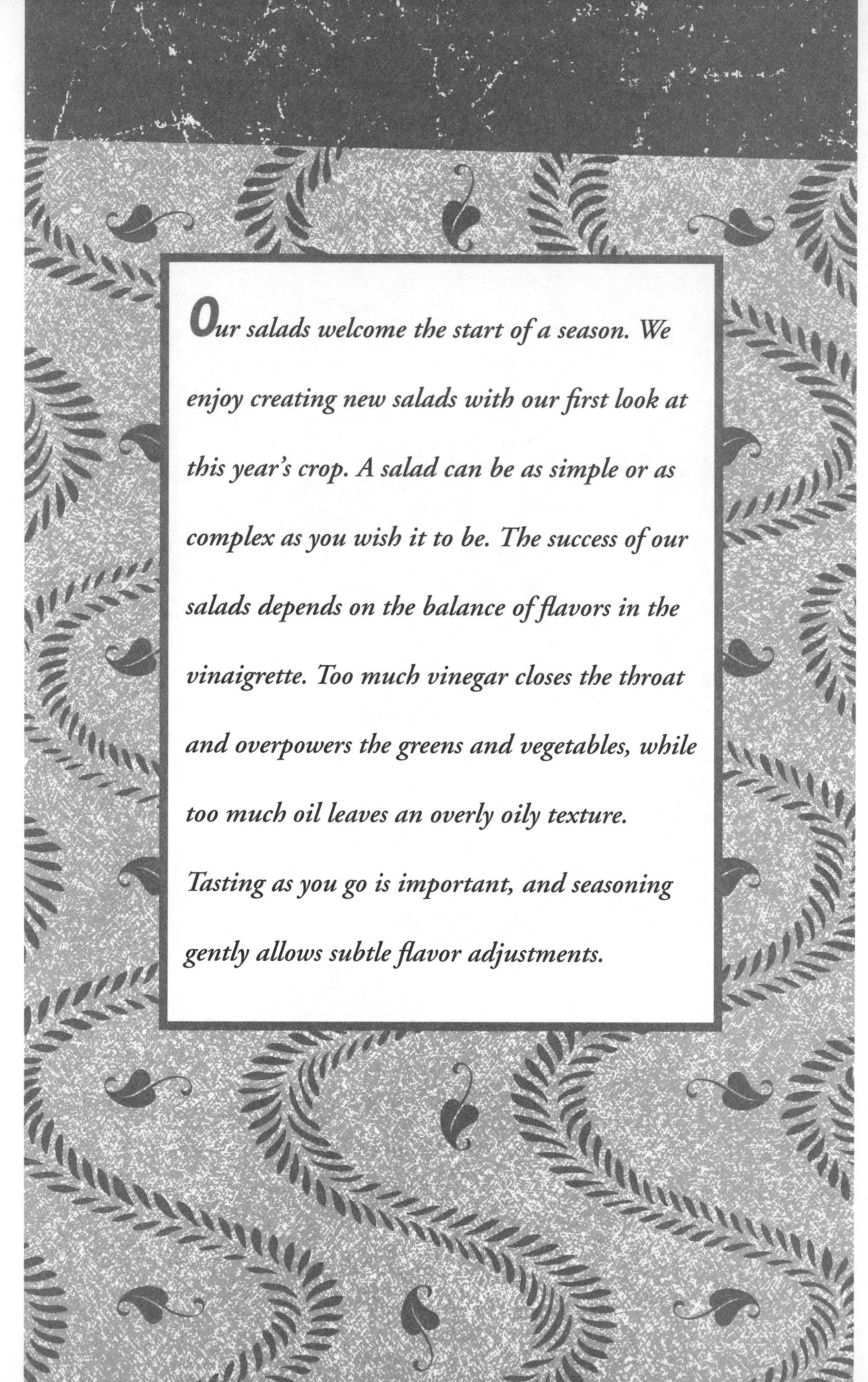

Our salads welcome the start of a season. We enjoy creating new salads with our first look at this year's crop. A salad can be as simple or as complex as you wish it to be. The success of our salads depends on the balance of flavors in the vinaigrette. Too much vinegar closes the throat and overpowers the greens and vegetables, while too much oil leaves an overly oily texture. Tasting as you go is important, and seasoning gently allows subtle flavor adjustments.

in the salad bowl

Simple Salad with Mustard Vinaigrette
Heirloom Tomato Salad with Feta and Balsamic Reduction
Grilled Asparagus Salad with Lemon-Thyme Vinaigrette
Green and Yellow Bean Salad with Peas and Sherry-Truffle Vinaigrette
Roasted Baby Beet and Blood Orange Salad with Champagne Vinaigrette
Grilled Fig Salad with Fig and Port Vinaigrette
Endive Salad with Pears and Blue Cheese with Pomegranate Vinaigrette
Salad of Figs, Candied Walnuts, and Gorgonzola Cheese
Grilled Quail Salad with Hazelnut Vinaigrette

Simple Salad with Mustard Vinaigrette

Serves 6

This is our version of what most restaurants call a "house salad." We call it a "simple salad" because of its fresh, simple flavors. We have adjusted this salad over the years, but this is the recipe that has stuck. It complements almost any large plate offered in this book.

6 cups mesclun greens, such as arugula, mâche, radicchio, or oakleaf
½ pound haricots verts, blanched (green beans may be substituted)
1 cup radishes, thinly sliced
1 cup olives, pitted (preferably Lucques or Niçoise)
1 cup Mustard Vinaigrette (recipe follows)

In a large bowl, mix all the ingredients together. Serve in a large bowl or on individual plates.

Mustard Vinaigrette

Makes 1 cup

- 2 tablespoons orange juice
- 2 tablespoons minced shallots
- 2 tablespoons chopped fresh tarragon
- 1 tablespoon Dijon mustard
- 2 tablespoons whole-grain mustard
- 1½ tablespoons honey
- ¼ cup Champagne vinegar
- ½ cup blended oil (page 7)
- salt and pepper

Mix the orange juice, shallots, and tarragon together in a small bowl. Whisk in the mustards, honey, and vinegar and slowly whisk in the oil. Season with salt and pepper.

Wine pairing Lillet blanc, Roussanne

Heirloom Tomato Salad with Feta and Balsamic Reduction

Serves 6

My fondest memories of tomatoes are of my mom and her green thumb. When I was a teenager, she had the perfect shore house in Margate, New Jersey, with four tomato plants in her backyard. I still remember the way those tomatoes tasted. When the first tomatoes were the size of a baseball, still greenish red and not quite ripe, I would dust them with cornmeal and seasonings and fry them in oil. I served them with steamed clams and corn on the cob.

6 to 8 heirloom tomatoes, any variety, cut into ¼-inch slices
4 basil leaves, torn
4 opal basil leaves, torn
6 mint leaves, torn
½ red onion, halved and very thinly sliced
3 tablespoons extra virgin olive oil
gray sea salt
freshly ground pepper
½ cup Balsamic Reduction (recipe follows)
¼ cup crumbled feta
cracked pepper

In a stainless steel bowl, gently toss the tomatoes with the basils, mint, red onion, olive oil, sea salt, and pepper. Drizzle the Balsamic Reduction on a plate and stack the tomatoes in the center. Crumble the feta around the tomatoes and top with the cracked pepper.

Balsamic Reduction

MAKES ½ CUP

3 cups balsamic vinegar

In a saucepan, over medium heat, slowly reduce the balsamic vinegar to ½ cup. Cool and use as desired.

WINE PAIRING **Roussanne**

Grilled Asparagus Salad with Lemon-Thyme Vinaigrette

Serves 6

Spring asparagus are so flavorful that it really isn't necessary to do too much to them. This recipe calls for blanching and grilling the asparagus; the blanch will soften them a little and preserve the color, and the grill will add a nice toasty flavor. We occasionally add spears of ripe white asparagus early in the season while they are available.

36 asparagus spears, trimmed and blanched
¼ cup olive oil
¼ teaspoon salt
¼ teaspoon white pepper
½ cup pistachios, toasted
1 cup Lemon-Thyme Vinaigrette (recipe follows)

Toss the asparagus with the olive oil, salt, and pepper. Place the asparagus on a hot grill and cook until well colored but not overcooked, 1 to 2 minutes per side. Toss the grilled asparagus and pistachios with the vinaigrette. Divide the asparagus among individual plates.

Lemon-Thyme Vinaigrette

MAKES 1¾ CUPS

- ½ pound bacon, julienned
- 2 tablespoons minced shallots
- 2 tablespoons chopped fresh lemon thyme or thyme
- ½ tablespoon minced garlic
- ½ cup Champagne vinegar
- 2 tablespoons grated lemon zest
- 1 cup blended oil (page 7)
- salt and white pepper

Cook the bacon in a sauté pan over medium heat until crisp. In a bowl, combine the hot bacon with the bacon fat, shallots, lemon thyme, and garlic and stir until the shallots are softened. Add the Champagne vinegar and lemon zest and slowly stir in the oil. Season with salt and pepper.

WINE PAIRING Roussanne

Green and Yellow Bean Salad with Peas and Sherry-Truffle Vinaigrette

SERVES 6

In season, beans grow like crazy. Though we are particularly fond of haricots verts, the basic garden varieties of Blue Lake and yellow wax beans make for a terrific salad. Be sure to thinly slice and julienne the prosciutto and mix it well with the other ingredients so that with every bite you taste bean as well as the cured meat. Our Sherry-Truffle Vinaigrette adds an earthy essence to this salad.

1 pound green beans, blanched and chilled
1 pound yellow wax beans, blanched and chilled
1 cup fresh English peas, shelled, blanched, and chilled
½ pound prosciutto, julienned
3 cups watercress, well washed, leaves only
1 cup Sherry-Truffle Vinaigrette (recipe follows)
salt and pepper

Combine the green and yellow beans, peas, prosciutto, watercress, and vinaigrette in a bowl and toss well. Season with salt and pepper.

Sherry-Truffle Vinaigrette

Makes 1 cup

⅓ cup blended oil (page 7)
1 tablespoon minced garlic
¼ cup sherry vinegar
⅓ cup simple syrup (page 8)
2 tablespoons truffle oil
salt and pepper

In a small sauté pan, combine the blended oil and garlic. Cook slowly over low heat; do not let the garlic brown. Remove from the heat and let steep for 30 minutes. Strain and discard the garlic.

In a bowl, combine the sherry vinegar and syrup. Slowly whisk in the garlic oil and truffle oil. Taste and adjust with salt, pepper, and syrup.

Wine pairing **Marsanne**

Food for thought *If you do not care for the truffle flavor, substitute another dressing for this salad. Either the Mustard Vinaigrette (page 89) or the Champagne Vinaigrette (page 97) would be delicious.*

Roasted Baby Beet and Blood Orange Salad with Champagne Vinaigrette

Serves 6

Baby beets are so beautiful. Although raw beets look rough and rugged, once they are roasted, peeled, and sliced, the medley of color among the Chioggas, goldens, and deep reds is just gorgeous. We like the combination of the sweet beets and tart blood oranges. The oranges complement the beets nicely and add another striking color.

- 36 to 40 baby beets, washed and with stems removed
- ¼ cup olive oil
- ½ cup Champagne Vinaigrette (recipe follows)
- 3 blood oranges, segments only (oranges or grapefruit may be substituted)
- 3 fresh tarragon sprigs, leaves only
- ¼ cup fresh Italian parsley, leaves only
- ½ pound watercress, well washed, leaves only
- salt and pepper
- ¼ pound hard cheese, such as dry Gouda or Parmesan, thinly shaved
- zest of 1 lemon, grated

Preheat the oven to 350°F.

Place the beets in a roasting pan and toss with the olive oil. Cover with foil and roast for 1½ hours. Let cool. Peel off the skins and cut the beets into quarters or halves, depending on the size of the beets.

In a large bowl, toss the beets with the vinaigrette, blood oranges, herbs, and watercress and season with salt and pepper. Serve in a large bowl and garnish with the shaved cheese and lemon zest.

Champagne Vinaigrette

MAKES ½ CUP

2½ tablespoons Champagne vinegar
1 teaspoon minced shallots
1 teaspoon Dijon mustard
2 teaspoons sugar
5 tablespoons extra virgin olive oil
salt and pepper

Combine the Champagne vinegar, shallots, mustard, and sugar in a bowl. Slowly whisk in the olive oil. Season with salt and pepper.

WINE PAIRING **Grenache**

FOOD FOR THOUGHT *For an elegant presentation, serve this salad in a Vella Cheese Crisp bowl (page 35) and omit the shaved cheese.*

Grilled Fig Salad with Fig and Port Vinaigrette

SERVES 6

Many guests have asked me how I came up with the name "the girl & the fig." I have certainly made up many stories over the years, but this salad sums up my philosophy of the restaurant. The fig is my symbol for passion—a passion for the ever-changing landscapes, the array of fruits and vegetables from the nearby farms, and the many vineyards that make up the Sonoma wine country. The Grilled Fig Salad, which has become our signature dish, encompasses the wine country simply by combining ingredients that are wonderful on their own yet when served together create entirely different flavors. These are the flavors of the earth, of the wine country terroir.

½ pound pancetta, diced
12 fresh figs, halved
6 bunches baby arugula
1 cup pecans, toasted
1 cup crumbled goat cheese (preferably Laura Chenel Chèvre)
1½ cups Fig and Port Vinaigrette (recipe follows)
pepper

In a small sauté pan, sauté the pancetta over medium heat until crisp. Set the pancetta aside, reserving the "oil." Brush the figs with the pancetta "oil." Grill the figs for 45 seconds on each side.

In a stainless steel bowl, toss the arugula, pecans, pancetta, and goat cheese with the vinaigrette. Place the salad on chilled plates and surround with grilled figs. Grind pepper over each salad with a pepper mill.

Fig and Port Vinaigrette

Makes 1½ cups

3 dried Black Mission figs
1 cup ruby port
¼ cup red wine vinegar
½ tablespoon minced shallots
¼ cup blended oil (page 7)
salt and pepper

Rehydrate the figs in the port until soft.

In a saucepan, reduce the port over medium heat to ½ cup.

Puree the figs, port, and vinegar in a food processor. Add the shallots and slowly whisk in the oil. Season with salt and pepper.

Wine pairing **Roussanne, Grenache Rosé**

Food for thought *If fresh figs are not in season, substitute good-quality moist figs (Brown Turkey figs are my favorite). I do not recommend grilling dried figs; just cut into small pieces and toss with the other salad ingredients.*

Endive Salad with Pears and Blue Cheese with Pomegranate Vinaigrette

Serves 6

Point Reyes Original Blue Cheese adds an interesting flavor dimension to this winter salad. Its salty flavor and creamy texture complement the endive and contrast with the citrus. If you are unable to find this cheese, you may substitute another blue cheese such as Roquefort, Maytag Blue, or Spanish Cabrales.

- 3 heads endive
- 3 oranges, segmented
- 3 grapefruits, segmented
- ½ pound mixed greens
- 1 cup Candied Walnuts (recipe follows)
- 2 Bosc pears, diced
- 1 cup Pomegranate Vinaigrette (recipe follows)
- ¼ pound blue cheese (preferably Point Reyes Original Blue)
- ¼ cup pomegranate seeds (optional)
- cracked pepper

Remove the heart at the bottom of each endive and slice it into ½-inch pieces.

In a large mixing bowl, combine the endive leaves and hearts, the orange and grapefruit segments, greens, walnuts, pears, vinaigrette, and blue cheese. Mix well.

Garnish with pomegranate seeds and crack fresh pepper over the salads before serving.

Candied Walnuts

MAKES 1 CUP

1 cup blended oil (page 7)
1 cup walnuts
3 tablespoons simple syrup (page 8)
pinch of salt
pinch of white pepper
pinch of cinnamon
pinch of nutmeg, freshly grated

Preheat the oven to 350°F.

Heat the oil over medium-low heat and fry the walnuts until golden brown, 4 to 5 minutes. Drain the walnuts on paper towels.

In a bowl, combine the nuts and syrup and toss to coat. Add the salt, pepper, and spices and toss again. Bake until the nuts are dried, 3 to 4 minutes.

Pomegranate Vinaigrette

MAKES 1¼ CUPS

¾ cup pomegranate juice
2 tablespoons chopped candied ginger
1 tablespoon minced shallots
3 tablespoons grapefruit juice
¼ cup red wine vinegar
½ teaspoon honey
½ cup blended oil (page 7)
salt and pepper

Place the juice and ginger in a saucepan and reduce by half. Place the reduced mixture in a blender and puree. Add the shallots, grapefruit juice, vinegar, and honey and pulse until well mixed. Slowly add the oil. Season with salt and pepper.

WINE PAIRING **Grenache**

FOOD FOR THOUGHT ***Double the recipe for Candied Walnuts and you will have some treats on hand to snack on or to serve with cocktails.***

Salad of Figs, Candied Walnuts, and Gorgonzola Cheese

SERVES 6

If you can find a creamy mountain Gorgonzola cheese, it will really enhance this salad. Mountain Gorgonzola crumbles easily and gently coats the field greens. If you cannot find it, don't fret; the salad will still taste great with your favorite blue.

- **¼ cup balsamic vinegar**
- **½ cup extra virgin olive oil**
- **½ teaspoon lemon juice**
- **salt and pepper**
- **6 cups mesclun greens, such as arugula, oak leaf, mâche, or radicchio**
- **½ cup crumbled mountain Gorgonzola**
- **12 fresh figs, halved**
- **⅓ cup Candied Walnuts (page 101)**

Mix together the balsamic vinegar, olive oil, lemon juice, salt, and pepper in a small bowl. In a separate bowl combine the greens, Gorgonzola, figs, and walnuts. Toss with the dressing and season with salt and pepper.

WINE PAIRING **Grenache Rosé or Cinsault**

FOOD FOR THOUGHT *Grilling the figs (see page 98) will add a toasty flavor to this salad.*

Grilled Quail Salad with Hazelnut Vinaigrette

Serves 6

This is a simple, elegant recipe that highlights autumn ingredients with contrasting textures and flavors. Try to get a nice even crisping of the skin when grilling the quail and choose ripe crisp pears, such as Asian or Bosc pears.

Marinade

½ cup red wine
zest of 1 lemon, grated
1 tablespoon minced garlic
1 tablespoon chopped fresh thyme
1 tablespoon chopped fresh Italian parsley
1 tablespoon chopped fresh sage
1 tablespoon honey
1 tablespoon whole-grain mustard
⅔ cup blended oil (page 7)
cracked pepper

6 quail, boned
olive oil

The salad

3 heads butter lettuce
½ cup hazelnuts, toasted, skinned, and chopped
3 pears, sliced
1 cup Hazelnut Vinaigrette (recipe follows)
cracked pepper

Combine the marinade ingredients in a bowl. Pour over the quail and toss to coat well. Allow the quail to marinate in a glass bowl for at least 2 hours in the refrigerator.

Heat a grill and brush with olive oil. Grill the quail 3 to 4 minutes on each side or until the skin is well browned but the meat still pink. Set aside and let cool. Cut each quail in half lengthwise through the breast.

In a large salad bowl, toss the lettuce, hazelnuts, pears, and vinaigrette. In individual bowls, arrange the salad and top each bowl with a portion of the grilled quail. Crack fresh pepper over each salad and serve.

Hazelnut Vinaigrette

Makes 1 cup

¼ cup Champagne vinegar
½ tablespoon honey
1 tablespoon minced shallots
2 tablespoons hazelnut oil
½ cup blended oil (page 7)
¼ cup toasted hazelnuts, roughly chopped
salt and pepper

Whisk the vinegar, honey, and shallots together in a small bowl. Slowly add the oils and whisk in the hazelnuts. Season with salt and pepper.

Wine pairing **Grenache Rosé or a Tavel**

Food for thought ***Serve this salad with a crusty loaf of bread and a wedge of blue cheese.***

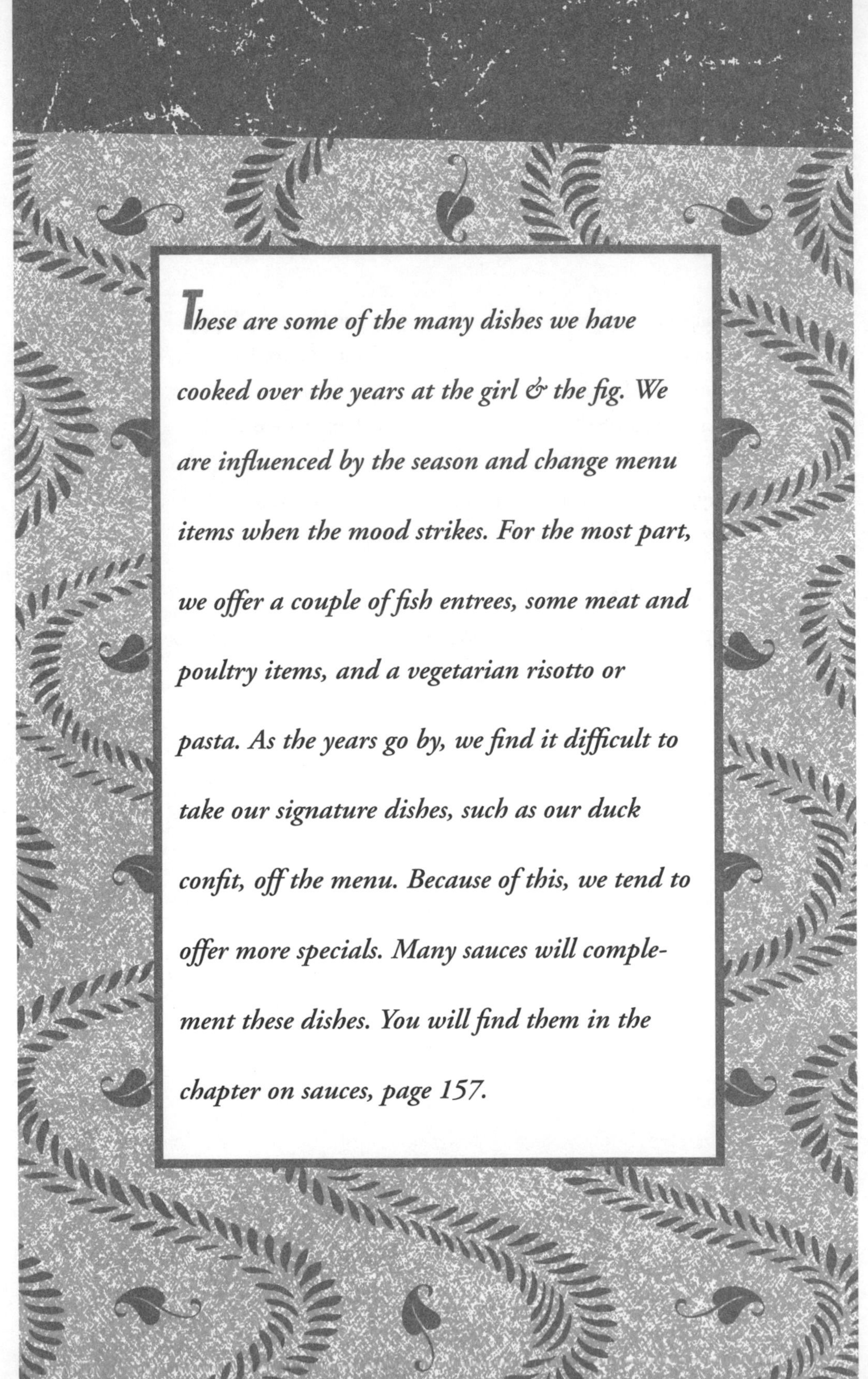

These are some of the many dishes we have cooked over the years at the girl & the fig. We are influenced by the season and change menu items when the mood strikes. For the most part, we offer a couple of fish entrees, some meat and poultry items, and a vegetarian risotto or pasta. As the years go by, we find it difficult to take our signature dishes, such as our duck confit, off the menu. Because of this, we tend to offer more specials. Many sauces will complement these dishes. You will find them in the chapter on sauces, page 157.

large plates

Summer Pasta

Serves 6

This relatively quick and easy recipe incorporates the favorite flavors of summer. Use ripe cherry and yellow pear tomatoes with summer baby squash, such as pattypan or baby zucchini. Use a pasta with a shape, such as penne or gemelli, rather than a spaghetti-like pasta.

1 pound cooked pasta
⅓ cup plus 2 tablespoons extra virgin olive oil
3 cups cherry tomatoes, cut in half
2 tablespoons minced garlic
⅓ cup chopped fresh basil
⅓ cup balsamic vinegar
¼ pound prosciutto, thinly sliced and julienned
5 ears white sweet corn, kernels removed
½ pound baby squash, blanched and cut into bite-size pieces
2 tablespoons Pistou (page 161)
salt and pepper
2 cups arugula
½ cup shaved Vella Dry Jack (see Sources, page 252; any hard cheese may be substituted)

Toss the pasta with 1 tablespoon of the olive oil. In a large bowl, combine the tomatoes, the eggplant if using, 1 tablespoon of the garlic, the basil, the ⅓ cup olive oil, and the balsamic vinegar. Set aside.

Heat the remaining tablespoon olive oil in a large sauté pan and sauté the prosciutto until it begins to crisp slightly. Add the corn and sauté until golden brown. Add the remaining 1 tablespoon garlic and sauté for 1 minute. Add the tomato mixture and squash and cook for 5 minutes over medium heat. Add the pasta and Pistou and mix well to warm the pasta through. Season with salt and pepper.

Place the arugula on the bottom of a large serving bowl and ladle the hot pasta on top. Stir gently and top with the shaved cheese.

Wine pairing **Roussanne**

Food for thought *Feel free to add other favorite vegetables of yours, such as eggplant, green beans, or peppers. Serve this pasta with Simple Salad (page 88) and crusty French bread.*

Pasta with Fromage Blanc, Brown Butter, Corn, and Spinach

Serves 6

Cowgirl Creamery's Fromage Blanc is rich and fresh yet light enough to balance the brown butter in this recipe. Fromage Blanc is a great substitute for ricotta in stuffed pasta such as ravioli. Herbs, vegetables, essences, and spices meld well with this cheese. Brown butter, corn, and spinach create a complex combination of flavors. The creamy caramel butter coats the pasta nicely and the salty prosciutto adds yet another dimension of flavor. These ingredients are also wonderful when served as a bed for scallops or grilled fish.

- ¼ pound (1 stick) unsalted butter
- 1 pound cooked pasta
- 1½ tablespoons blended oil (page 7)
- ½ pound prosciutto, julienned (pancetta or bacon may be substituted)
- 1 teaspoon minced garlic
- 4 ears white sweet corn, kernels removed
- 2 cups baby spinach
- salt and pepper
- ½ cup Fromage Blanc

To make the brown butter, heat the butter in a stainless steel pan over a low flame until golden to dark brown. (The flavor should be slightly sweet.) Strain the butter through cheesecloth and toss with the pasta. Keep warm.

In a large sauté pan, heat the oil. Sauté the prosciutto until crispy and add the garlic and corn. Sauté until the corn starts to turn brown, about 5 minutes. Add the spinach and stir well. Add the pasta and mix well to coat. Place the pasta in a large serving bowl. Season to taste. Mix well and top with crumbled Fromage Blanc.

Wine pairing Viognier or Marsanne

Wild Mushroom Risotto

Serves 6

If you love risotto and do not mind the tedious, constant stirring, you will adore this risotto recipe. Farmed mushrooms tend to be more delicate in flavor compared to some of the foraged mushrooms we get from Stephen, which are rich, earthy, and robust. If you can find lobster mushrooms, add them to your mushroom mixture. They add a unique flavor and brighten up an otherwise brown dish.

4 tablespoons blended oil (page 7)
2 cups trimmed and chopped wild mushrooms (such as cremini, portobello, or Chanterelle)
salt
1 tablespoon chopped fresh thyme
1 tablespoon chopped fresh oregano
1 cup minced onion
1 tablespoon minced garlic
2 cups Arborio rice
1 cup dry white wine
7 cups hot mushroom stock (page 10)
3 tablespoons unsalted butter, cut into pieces, at room temperature
1 cup grated Parmesan
2 tablespoons chopped fresh Italian parsley
pepper

Heat 2 tablespoons of the oil in a large sauté pan. Add the mushrooms, season with salt, and sauté for 5 minutes or so to evaporate the moisture and intensify the mushroom flavor. Add the thyme and oregano and mix well. Set aside.

Heat the remaining 2 tablespoons oil in another sauté pan and sauté the onion until translucent. Add the garlic and sauté for a minute more. Stir in the rice and lightly toast it by stirring slowly and fairly constantly with a wooden spoon over moderately high heat until the grains begin to turn lightly golden and smell toasted. Add the wine to the rice all at once and turn the heat up fairly high to allow the wine to evaporate. When the wine has almost evaporated and the rice is almost dry, ladle in enough hot stock to just cover the rice. Reduce the heat to a simmer, season with salt, and stir slowly and almost constantly for about 20 minutes. Continue to add the stock a little at a time as the rice absorbs it.

After the rice has cooked for about 8 minutes, stir in the sautéed mushroom mixture. Ladle ½ cup stock into the pan the mushrooms were sautéed in to deglaze the pan and add the liquid to the rice.

When the risotto is ready (the rice grains will have doubled in size and be suspended in a creamy liquid and the rice should be just tender), remove it from the heat. With a wooden spoon, immediately stir in the butter and ½ cup of the cheese. Add the parsley and season with pepper. Sprinkle with the remaining cheese.

WINE PAIRING **Viognier or Grenache**
FOOD FOR THOUGHT *Wild Mushroom Risotto is a really great side dish for many of our large plates, such as Grilled Mahi Mahi (page 120), Grilled Chicken Breasts (page 126), or Pan-Seared Beef Fillet (page 150). It is also wonderful on its own.*

the mushroom man

Stephen Scallopino, Glen Ellen, California

Many people would be envious of Stephen's happy-go-lucky attitude. He is our forager, our revered mushroom man, our god of dirt and fungus. When Stephen is around town, we know that we are about to get some great mushrooms!

He showed up on our back porch about four years ago, like a traveling mushroom salesman. I think I may have shooed him away. Who would have thought that buying mushrooms out of someone's car was the way to taste the real flavor of the forest? I was a bit leery of him, in case he was selling "magic mushrooms." Stephen's mushrooms aren't those magic mushrooms, but I must say they put a spell on our cooking. They turn risotto into Creamy Risotto with Flecks of Chanterelles and Wood Ear Gravy. They turn a mushroom ragout into Medley of Forest Mushrooms over Camellia Cheese. I was skeptical when he brought in the lobster mushrooms; they don't taste like lobster, but their vivid reddish-orange hue was more than worthy of our Crispy Sweetbreads over Wilted Greens.

Lobster-Scented Risotto

SERVES 6

Our lobster stock is so intensely flavored that it seems as if you are eating fresh lobster with every bite. Unless we are using lobster meat in a special dish, we order lobster culls (bodies) for roasting. They make a wonderful stock at a reasonable price. If you are lucky enough to have whole lobsters on hand, reserve the meat and add it to the risotto.

- 6 cups lobster stock (page 12)
- 2 tablespoons blended oil (page 7)
- 1 large onion, finely diced
- 1 fennel bulb, diced
- 2 cups Arborio rice
- 2 tablespoons chopped fresh Italian parsley
- 1 tablespoon chopped fresh tarragon
- 1 tablespoon chopped fresh thyme
- 1 cup dry white wine
- ¼ pound (1 stick) unsalted butter
- salt and pepper

Bring the lobster stock to a boil, reduce the heat, and keep warm.

In a large sauté pan, heat the oil over medium heat and sauté the onion and fennel until soft. Add the rice and herbs and cook for 10 minutes over medium heat, stirring constantly. Add the wine and let cook until the wine evaporates and the rice is almost dry, 2 to 3 minutes. Add 2 cups of the lobster stock and stir constantly until absorbed. Continue until you have used all of the stock. (The total cooking time should be about 30 minutes.) Mix in the butter and season with salt and pepper to taste.

WINE PAIRING **Roussanne**

FOOD FOR THOUGHT *Everyone has an opinion about the way risotto should be cooked; we prefer ours slightly al dente.*

Pan-Seared Scallops with Orange-Tarragon Beurre Blanc

SERVES 6

I first learned how to make a beurre blanc at The Restaurant School in Philadelphia. This was one of my favorite sauces. It is quick and easy and boosts the flavor of fish and poultry. A beurre blanc must be made to order because it is a delicate sauce that will not keep for long without breaking. You can easily vary it with fruit juice and your favorite herbs—oregano, thyme, and tarragon are all nice additions, while orange and pineapple juice change the essence of the sauce.

3 tablespoons olive oil
24 sea scallops
salt and pepper
1 cup Orange-Tarragon Beurre Blanc (recipe follows)

Heat the olive oil in a large skillet. Sear the scallops quickly over high heat until golden brown all over. Add salt and pepper to taste. Keep the scallops warm while you make the sauce, then drizzle with the beurre blanc.

Orange-Tarragon Beurre Blanc

Makes 1 cup

1 tablespoon minced shallots
1 tablespoon white wine vinegar
1 tablespoon Grand Marnier
1½ tablespoons fresh orange juice
1 tablespoon chopped fresh tarragon
½ cup heavy cream
½ pound (2 sticks) unsalted butter, cut into ½-inch cubes, at room temperature
1 teaspoon chopped orange zest
salt and white pepper

Combine the shallots, vinegar, Grand Marnier, orange juice, and tarragon in a saucepan and cook rapidly over high heat until the liquid has almost evaporated, 1 to 2 minutes. Reduce the heat to medium, add the cream, and cook until the mixture has reduced and thickened slightly, 1 to 2 minutes. Remove the pan from the heat and set it aside until you are ready to serve the sauce.

Just before serving, add the butter to the pan, whisking constantly over very low heat. Add the orange zest and season with salt and white pepper.

Wine pairing **Marsanne**

Food for thought *These scallops will also work very well with Caper Vinaigrette (page 117), Fire-Roasted Tomato Vinaigrette (page 121), Roasted Tomato and Garlic Sauce (page 165), and Saffron Cream Sauce (page 168). Serve them with a side of Citrus Pearl Couscous (page 194) or Wilted Greens (page 177).*

Pan-Roasted Halibut with Caper Vinaigrette

SERVES 6

Our local halibut season runs from spring to summer and the fish arrive large and very fresh. The flavor of local halibut is richer than the Alaskan halibut we use the rest of the year. For this dish, we like our halibut to have a very crispy skin, which we achieve only by using an extremely hot pan that burns the seasonings into the skin and locks in the juices. When you achieve this crispiness, the texture is exquisite.

6 halibut fillets (6 to 8 ounces each)
salt and white pepper
1½ tablespoons olive oil
Caper Vinaigrette (recipe follows)

Preheat the oven to 350°F.

Gently season the halibut on both sides with salt and white pepper. Heat the oil in an ovenproof sauté pan and sear the halibut on one side until lightly brown. Flip the fish over and sear the other side. Flip over again and place the pan in the oven to cook for 6 to 8 minutes. Drizzle with the Caper Vinaigrette.

Caper Vinaigrette

Makes 1 cup

- 2 egg yolks
- 2 teaspoons lemon juice
- 1 teaspoon minced garlic
- 2 teaspoons Champagne vinegar
- ½ cup blended oil (page 7)
- 2 tablespoons capers, drained
- 1 tablespoon whole-grain mustard
- 1 teaspoon chopped fresh tarragon
- 2 teaspoons chopped fresh thyme
- 2 teaspoons chopped fresh Italian parsley
- salt and pepper

In a food processor or in a blender, combine the egg yolks, lemon juice, garlic, and vinegar. Slowly whisk in the oil. Remove the mixture from the blender to a bowl and fold in the capers, mustard, and herbs. Season with salt and pepper. Drizzle the vinaigrette over the halibut.

Wine pairing Roussanne

Food for thought *Pan-roasted halibut also works well with Citrus Beurre Blanc (page 166), Fire-Roasted Tomato Vinaigrette (page 121), Sorrel Sauce (page 169), and Saffron Cream Sauce (page 168). Serve with a side of Fingerling Potato Confit (page 189), Haricots Verts (page 173), Citrus Pearl Couscous (page 194), or Wilted Greens (page 177).*

Broiled Halibut with Spring Vegetable Ragout

Serves 6

In keeping with our rustic country-French approach, a simple ragout is a great way for us to express ourselves. Ragouts incorporate seasonal vegetables, while the method builds flavor. We put this dish on the menu to celebrate spring as soon as we see the first fava beans of the season. Use fresh morels if you can.

¼ cup fresh Italian parsley (leaves only)
¼ cup chicken stock (page 11)
⅓ cup plus 2 tablespoons extra virgin olive oil
salt and pepper
2 tablespoons unsalted butter
2 teaspoons minced garlic
1 tablespoon minced shallots
2 cups sliced wild mushrooms
2 cups scallions, white and green parts, sliced on the diagonal
1 tablespoon chopped fresh thyme
1 tablespoon chopped fresh oregano
2 tablespoons dry white wine
1 cup blanched and peeled fava beans
1½ pounds red potatoes, boiled and sliced
6 halibut fillets (6 to 8 ounces each)
1½ teaspoons truffle oil or Saffron Butter (page 158)

Blend the parsley, chicken stock, and the ⅓ cup olive oil in a food processor and season with salt and pepper. Set aside.

Heat a sauté pan and melt the butter. Sauté the garlic and shallots until soft, then add the mushrooms and scallions. Cook the mushrooms for 5 minutes, stirring constantly. Add the thyme and oregano. Deglaze the pan with the white wine and add the fava beans and potatoes. Add the parsley-oil mixture and adjust the seasoning. Set aside and keep warm.

In another pan, place the halibut and brush it with the 2 tablespoons olive oil and season with salt and pepper. Under a hot broiler, broil the halibut for 2 to 3 minutes on each side or until firm. Serve the halibut in a large bowl with the ragout and drizzle with the truffle oil or a slice of Saffron Butter, if you prefer.

Wine pairing **Roussanne**

Pan-Roasted Monkfish with Clams, White Beans, and Wild Mushrooms

Serves 6

This is a winter ragout. The earthy richness of the mushrooms, the beans, and the sausage complement the dense texture of the monkfish. Monkfish is meaty, not flaky like snapper or sea bass, and lends itself to this hearty ragout.

- 3 tablespoons blended oil (page 7)
- ¾ pound pork sausage, cut in ½-inch slices (sautéed chopped pancetta or Applewood smoked bacon may be substituted)
- 2 cups sliced wild mushrooms
- 2 tablespoons minced shallots
- 2 tablespoons minced garlic
- 24 manila clams (in the shell)
- ¾ cup dry white wine
- ½ cup chicken stock (page 11)
- 2 teaspoons chopped fresh thyme
- 2 teaspoons chopped fresh Italian parsley
- 1 cup white beans cooked and seasoned with salt and pepper
- 2 teaspoons lemon juice
- salt and pepper
- 2 tablespoons unsalted butter, cut in pieces
- 6 monkfish fillets (8 to 10 ounces each)
- fresh Italian parsley leaves

Preheat the oven to 350°F.

Heat 1 tablespoon of the oil in a large sauté pan over medium-high heat, add the sausage, and cook until brown. Add the mushrooms, shallots, garlic, and clams and mix well. Add the white wine, chicken stock, thyme, parsley, cooked beans, and lemon juice, and season with salt and pepper. Simmer until the clams open. Finish the dish with the butter and keep warm.

In an ovenproof pan, heat the remaining 2 tablespoons oil until very hot. Season the monkfish with salt and pepper and sear all over. Transfer the pan to the oven and roast for 10 minutes. (The fish will be firm when cooked.) Place each piece of monkfish in a bowl, smother it with sauce, and garnish with the parsley.

Wine pairing Grenache

Grilled Mahi Mahi with Fire-Roasted Tomato Vinaigrette

Serves 6

Mahi mahi cooks quickly on your outdoor grill. This fish has a subtle flavor and works nicely with many sauces. The Fire-Roasted Tomato Vinaigrette is a fresh sauce with ample acidity that complements the mahi mahi. Though the recipe calls for Roma tomatoes, if you have garden-ripe heirlooms, use them to intensify the tomato flavor. This is a summer sauce that shines with the fresh flavors of your herb garden.

1 tablespoon olive oil
6 mahi mahi fillets (6 to 8 ounces each)
salt and white pepper
Fire-Roasted Tomato Vinaigrette (recipe follows)

Gently brush the olive oil on both sides of the mahi mahi and season with salt and white pepper. Grill the fillets over high heat for about 3 minutes on each side. Drizzle with the vinaigrette.

Fire-Roasted Tomato Vinaigrette

MAKES 2 CUPS

- 1 pound Roma tomatoes, cut in half lengthwise and seeds removed
- 1 cup extra virgin olive oil
- salt and pepper
- 1 teaspoon minced garlic
- 1 tablespoon minced shallots
- 1 tablespoon honey
- 1 tablespoon whole-grain mustard
- ¼ cup sherry vinegar
- 2 tablespoons chopped fresh Italian parsley
- 1 teaspoon chopped fresh oregano
- 1 tablespoon chopped fresh basil

Heat a stovetop grill pan or an outdoor grill.

Toss the tomatoes with the olive oil and salt and pepper. Cook them skin side down on the grill until the skin is black. Remove 1 tablespoon of the tomato oil remaining in the bowl after tossing and reserve the rest. Heat the 1 tablespoon tomato oil in a skillet over high heat and sauté the garlic and shallots until soft. Add the tomatoes and mix well, and sauté the mixture until the tomatoes are soft. Remove from the heat and cool the tomatoes in the refrigerator.

Place the cooled tomatoes, the honey, whole-grain mustard, sherry vinegar, and reserved tomato oil in a food processor or blender. Pulse to incorporate the ingredients. Adjust the seasoning and add the herbs. Drizzle over the mahi mahi. The vinaigrette will keep in the refrigerator for 7 days.

WINE PAIRING **Roussanne**

FOOD FOR THOUGHT *Grilled Mahi Mahi also works well with Orange-Tarragon Beurre Blanc (page 115), Tomato Cream Sauce (page 167), Sorrel Sauce (page 169), Saffron Butter (page 158), and Warm Chive Vinaigrette (page 162). Serve this dish with a side of Citrus Pearl Couscous (page 194), Haricots Verts (page 173), Roasted Asparagus (page 174), or Braised Leeks (page 181).*

Fig Leaf–Wrapped Rainbow Trout Stuffed with Lavender, Fennel, and Herbs

SERVES 6

Looking at a fig tree, I see not only the luscious ripened figs of summer, but the beautiful leaves that grow into perfect adornments for plate or table. Each fig tree has uniquely shaped leaves. As well as using fig leaves to grace our cheese platters, we use them as wrappers in which to steam fish and grill goat cheese.

In this recipe the fig leaf perfumes the trout and complements the flavors of the lavender, leeks, and fennel.

12 large fig leaves (see Sources, page 253)
1 tablespoon blended oil (page 7)
1 fennel bulb, thinly sliced
1 leek, white part only, julienned
3 tablespoons chopped fresh thyme
1 tablespoon chopped fresh oregano
6 whole rainbow trout (8 to 10 ounces each)
salt and pepper
about 12 lavender sprigs plus 3 tablespoons chopped fresh lavender blossoms or ½ tablespoon dried lavender
2 lemons, thinly sliced

Preheat the oven to 400°F.

Blanch the fig leaves in boiling salted water for 3 to 5 minutes until limp and pliable. Shock in an ice bath and set aside.

Heat the oil in a large pan and sauté the fennel and leek with the thyme and oregano until soft.

Rinse the trout inside and out and season lightly with salt and pepper. Layer the inside of each trout with 1 or 2 lavender sprigs, a few tablespoons of the sautéed fennel mixture, and 2 or 3 slices of lemon, and season with salt and pepper.

Wrap each trout tightly with 2 fig leaves; the smooth side of the leaf should be touching the fish. Place the trout in a baking dish and add enough water to cover the bottom half inch of the dish. Cover the dish with foil, place in the oven, and poach for 35 minutes.

When the fish is cooked, open the fig leaves slightly and garnish with lavender blossoms. Serve immediately.

WINE PAIRING Roussanne

The proper way to eat a fig, in society,
Is to split it in four, holding it by the stump,
And open it, so that it is a glittering, rosy, moist, honied,
heavy-petalled four-petalled flower.

D. H. LAWRENCE, "FIGS"

Grilled Salmon with Lavender Beurre Rouge

Serves 6

The old cliché of serving white wine with fish and red wine with meat encouraged some experimentation in our kitchen. Adding garden-fresh lavender to traditional beurre rouge was a successful trial. We serve this sauce with grilled salmon, a fattier fish often accompanied by red wine. A red or white wine will pair nicely. (Salmon may also be baked in the oven.)

1 tablespoon olive oil
6 salmon fillets (6 to 8 ounces each)
salt and white pepper
1½ cups Lavender Beurre Rouge (recipe follows)

Gently brush the olive oil on both sides of the salmon and season with salt and pepper. Grill the fillets over high heat for about 3 minutes on each side and drizzle with the beurre rouge.

Lavender Beurre Rouge

MAKES 1½ CUPS

2 tablespoons minced shallots
1 cup red wine
1 bay leaf
1 cup heavy cream
½ teaspoon dried lavender
½ pound (2 sticks) unsalted butter, cut into 1-inch cubes
salt and white pepper

In a saucepan, combine the shallots, wine, and bay leaf over medium heat. Reduce the liquid to ½ cup. Add the cream and lavender and reduce by half. Off the heat, gradually whisk in the butter, 3 or 4 pieces at a time. Be sure they are incorporated before adding more. Return the pan to the heat and season with salt and white pepper. Strain the sauce and serve.

WINE PAIRING **Grenache**

FOOD FOR THOUGHT *Grilled salmon can also be served with the following sauces: Citrus Beurre Blanc (page 166), Saffron Balsamic Essence (page 163), Sorrel Sauce (page 169), Roasted Tomato and Garlic Sauce (page 165), and Saffron Cream Sauce (page 168). Serve the salmon with a side dish of Orange-Scented Braised Endive (page 180), Basil-Scented Potato Cakes (page 190), Wilted Greens (page 177), or Roasted Potatoes (page 188).*

Grilled Chicken Breasts with Tarragon-Mustard Sauce

Serves 6

With the opening of our Petaluma location, our chicken dishes pay homage to the original Petaluma chicken ranchers. A local favorite chicken is called the "Rocky." "Rocky" chickens are raised solely by Petaluma Poultry on local ranches throughout Sonoma and Marin counties. All the ranches are located within thirty miles of Petaluma Poultry, just down the street from the Petaluma "fig." The chickens are raised on a soft bed of rice hulls, are fed a diet of corn and soy, and move about freely. For this dish, try to find organic chickens in your local market; the difference in taste is remarkable.

6 whole chicken breasts (10 to 12 ounces each)
3 tablespoons olive oil
salt and pepper
Tarragon-Mustard Sauce (recipe follows)

Brush the chicken breasts with the olive oil and season with salt and pepper. Using a grill or stovetop grill pan, grill the breasts over medium heat for 5 minutes on each side. Serve the breasts with a spoonful of mustard sauce.

Tarragon-Mustard Sauce

Makes 1 cup

1 teaspoon blended oil (page 7)
2 tablespoons minced shallots
3 tablespoons minced garlic
2 teaspoons chopped fresh tarragon
¼ cup white wine
¼ cup sherry
½ cup chicken stock (page 11)
½ cup heavy cream
pinch of turmeric
1 tablespoon Dijon mustard
2 tablespoons honey
3 tablespoons unsalted butter, cut in 1-inch cubes
salt and pepper

Heat the oil in a medium sauté pan and sauté the shallots and garlic until translucent, 2 to 3 minutes. Add the tarragon, white wine, and sherry. Reduce the liquid by half and add the chicken stock. Reduce by half again and slowly add the cream. Reduce the liquid to 1 cup. Add the turmeric, mustard, and honey and slowly whisk in the butter. Season the sauce with salt and pepper.

Wine pairing **Marsanne or Grenache**

Food for thought *Grilled Chicken Breasts will also work well with Roasted Tomato and Garlic Sauce (page 165), Pistou (page 161), Sonoma Mustard Sauce (page 147), Shallot and Red Wine Sauce (page 165), and also with Roasted Garlic Aïoli (page 159). Serve with a side of Wild Mushroom Ragout (page 182), Haricots Verts (page 173), Roasted Potatoes (page 188), or Roasted Cauliflower (page 175).*

Braised Chicken with Prunes, Olives, and Capers

Serves 6

This dish is a delicious combination of sweet and savory. It's a distinctive recipe that defines our style of cooking: simple and rustic, yet sophisticated. This recipe is always a crowd pleaser. Perfect for a cool rainy night with your favorite Grenache, the rich flavors of the sauce complement the dark meat of the chicken. When we serve this entrée in the restaurant, I call the prunes "dried plums" and we always sell out.

Marinade

- **6 chicken legs, drumsticks and thighs separated**
- **1 tablespoon minced garlic**
- **2 tablespoons chopped fresh thyme**
- **2 tablespoons chopped fresh tarragon**
- **2 tablespoons chopped fresh sage**
- **¼ cup Armagnac or other brandy**
- **¼ cup red wine vinegar**
- **¼ cup blended oil (page 7)**
- **½ teaspoon salt**
- **¼ teaspoon pepper**

Braise

- **2 tablespoons blended oil (page 7)**
- **1 cup white wine**
- **1½ cups pitted prunes, cut in half**
- **½ cup cracked and pitted green olives**
- **¼ cup capers with juice**
- **3 bay leaves**
- **1 cup chicken stock (page 11)**
- **¼ cup chopped fresh Italian parsley**
- **4 tablespoons (½ stick) unsalted butter**

To make the marinade, in a large bowl combine the chicken with the garlic, herbs, Armagnac, red wine vinegar, oil, salt, and pepper. Mix gently, cover, and marinate overnight. The next day, remove the chicken and discard the marinade.

Preheat the oven to 350°F.

To make the braise, heat the oil in a large shallow roasting pan over medium heat. Slowly sear the chicken, skin side down, until golden brown, about 5 minutes on each side. Remove any excess fat from the pan and deglaze the pan with the white wine. Add the prunes, olives, capers with juice, bay leaves, and chicken stock. Cover with foil and place the pan in the oven for about 30 minutes or until the chicken is 165°F or an instant-read thermometer.

Remove the chicken from the pan and keep warm. Bring the prune mixture to a simmer on the stovetop and add the parsley and butter. Simmer to meld the ingredients and adjust the seasoning if necessary. Return the chicken to the sauce and serve.

WINE PAIRING **Grenache**

FOOD FOR THOUGHT ***Rabbit, duck, or turkey can be substituted for the chicken. They will all work wonderfully. Serve this dish with Mashed Potatoes (page 191) or buttered egg noodles for a comforting winter dinner.***

Coq au Vin

Serves 6 to 8

On a cold winter night, nothing warms the soul better than a rich, luscious coq au vin. Give me a bowl of this and a chunk of baguette and I'm in heaven. This recipe calls for 7½ cups (about two bottles) of red wine. Use a wine that you like to drink; if you wouldn't want to drink it, you probably won't like the way it tastes in a sauce. A simple inexpensive French red should do the trick.

Marinade

- 1½ cups red wine
- ½ tablespoon chopped fresh Italian parsley
- 3 garlic cloves, chopped
- ½ cup blended oil (page 7)
- 2 teaspoons salt
- 2 bay leaves
- 2 tablespoons soy sauce

- 6 chicken legs
- 6 chicken thighs

- 2 pounds Yukon Gold potatoes, quartered

Braise

- 1 carrot, peeled and diced into large pieces
- 1 onion, diced into large pieces
- ½ bunch celery, diced into large pieces
- 2 tablespoons blended oil (page 7)
- ½ tablespoon black peppercorns
- 2 tablespoons tomato paste
- 1 tablespoon unsweetened cocoa powder
- ½ teaspoon cinnamon
- 4 cups red wine
- bouquet garni (4 thyme sprigs, 4 Italian parsley sprigs, 2 bay leaves)
- 6 cups chicken stock (page 11)

Sauté

- 2 cups flour
- salt and pepper
- ½ pound pancetta, diced
- 1 pound button mushrooms, trimmed and cleaned
- 2 tablespoons blended oil (page 7)
- 3 tablespoons Cognac
- 2 cups red wine
- 30 pearl onions, blanched and peeled

To make the marinade, mix the red wine, parsley, garlic, oil, salt, bay leaves, and soy sauce together in a large bowl big enough to accommodate the chicken. Add the chicken and marinate for at least 24 hours.

Preheat the oven to 400°F. Roast the potatoes for about 35 minutes or until soft. Set aside and turn off the oven.

To make the braise, in a stockpot slowly sauté the carrot, onion, and celery in the oil until the onion is lightly browned and soft. Add the peppercorns and tomato paste and cook until soft. Add the cocoa powder and cinnamon. Deglaze the pan with the red wine and reduce by half. Add the bouquet garni and chicken stock. Simmer for 1 hour and strain. (There should be 1 quart liquid remaining.)

Preheat the oven to 350°F.

For the sauté, remove the chicken from the marinade and pat dry. Discard the marinade. In a bowl, combine the flour and salt and pepper and dredge the chicken in it. Set aside.

Cook the pancetta until crisp in a heavy-bottomed ovenproof pan large enough to hold all the chicken. Remove the pancetta and set it aside, keeping the fat in the pan. Sauté the mushrooms in the pancetta fat until well browned and remove. In the same pan, sauté the chicken until well browned on both sides, about 5 minutes per side. (Add more oil if needed.)

Deglaze the pan, first with the Cognac and then with the red wine. Reduce the liquid by half. Add the reduced chicken stock, pancetta, mushrooms, and pearl onions and place the pan in the oven for about 20 minutes.

Remove the chicken to a platter and keep warm. Reduce the wine sauce by a third. Add the potatoes to the wine sauce and serve over the chicken.

WINE PAIRING **Cinsault, sparkling French cider, or beer**

Grilled Pork Chops with Apple Cider Sauce

Serves 6

Brining the pork chop is the most important part of this recipe. The brine adds another layer of flavor to the pork and helps to keep it juicy and tender. If you can find fresh unfiltered apple cider, use it to enhance the Apple Cider Sauce. I have two favorite sources for apple products: Martinelli, along Russian River Road, where they produce incredible ciders as well as award-winning wines, and The Apple Farm in Philo, about two hours north of Sonoma. Sally Schmidt makes an apple cider vinegar and an apple butter to die for!

Brine

3 bay leaves
½ tablespoon black peppercorns
1 clove
½ tablespoon crushed red pepper
¾ tablespoon dried thyme
1 tablespoon anise seed
1 cup sugar
¾ cup salt
1 tablespoon minced garlic

6 pork chops (10 ounces each)
Apple Cider Sauce (recipe follows)

In a spice grinder or with a mortar and pestle, grind the bay leaves, peppercorns, clove, red pepper, thyme, and anise seed to a fine powder.

In a large bowl, prepare a brine by mixing together 1 gallon water, the sugar, and the salt. Stir until the sugar and salt dissolve. Stir in the herb-spice mix and garlic. Cover the pork chops with the brine, cover bowl with wrap, and refrigerate for at least 30 hours.

Preheat a grill. Place the pork chops on the grill and cook for 5 to 7 minutes on each side, depending on their thickness. Keep the chops warm while you prepare the sauce.

Apple Cider Sauce

Yield 1¾ cups

- 1 tablespoon blended oil (page 7)
- 2 tablespoons minced shallots
- 1 tablespoon chopped fresh sage
- 2 Granny Smith apples, peeled, cored, and sliced
- ¾ cup unfiltered apple cider
- 2 tablespoons cider vinegar
- 2 cups chicken stock (page 11)
- salt and pepper
- 2 tablespoons unsalted butter, cut in pieces
- ¼ cup pistachios, toasted and coarsely chopped

To make the sauce, heat the oil and sauté the shallots in a saucepan over medium heat until they are translucent. Add the sage and apple slices and cook until the apples are soft and begin to brown, about 5 to 6 minutes. Add the cider, vinegar, and chicken stock and simmer until the liquid is reduced by half. Season with salt and pepper and set aside to cool. Puree the mixture in a blender and strain.

To serve, heat the sauce until it just begins to simmer. Remove from the heat and whisk in the butter and pistachios.

Wine pairing **Grenache Rosé or Grenache**

Food for thought *These pork chops are also excellent with the Tarragon-Mustard Sauce (page 127), Sonoma Mustard Sauce (page 147), or Dried Cherry and Green Peppercorn Sauce (page 166). On the side, serve the Apple-Yam Gratin (page 186), Red Chard, Cheddar, and Potato Gratin (page 187), Mashed Potatoes (page 191), or Roasted Baby Beets and Figs (page 178).*

Sonoma Rabbit Two Ways with Baby Artichoke Pan Sauce

SERVES 6

Last Easter, the chefs gave the bunnies a break and substituted chicken in this recipe. Usually, however, we use rabbit in this dish. The brine tenderizes an almost fatless rabbit leg, and after braising, the meat will be tender and juicy.

Brine

¼ cup sugar
¼ cup salt
1 tablespoon anise seed
2 tablespoons minced garlic
5 black peppercorns
1 bay leaf

3 rabbits, quartered, loins reserved

Braise

2 tablespoons blended oil (page 7)
1 cup apple cider
6 cups chicken stock (page 11)
½ medium onion, chopped

Sauce

2 tablespoons blended oil (page 7)
1½ pounds baby artichokes, cleaned, quartered, and blanched
½ teaspoon minced garlic
6 tablespoons unsalted butter, cut in pieces
salt and pepper

To make the brine, in a large bowl combine the sugar, salt, 6 cups water, the anise seed, garlic, peppercorns, and bay leaf. Add the rabbit (reserve the loins) and allow to marinate at least 24 hours in the refrigerator.

Preheat the oven to 350°F.

Remove the rabbit from the brine and pat dry. Discard the brine.

To make the braise, heat the oil and brown the rabbit legs on both sides in a large ovenproof pan. Deglaze the pan with the apple cider and add the chicken stock and onion. Cover with foil and bake for 45 minutes to 1 hour. Remove the rabbit and keep warm. On the stovetop, reduce the liquid to 3 cups.

To make the sauce, sear the rabbit loins in the oil in a large sauté pan. Remove and set aside. Add the artichokes to the pan and caramelize over medium heat. Add the garlic and cook for 30 seconds. Add the reduced braising liquid and rabbit loins. Reduce the liquid by half. Add the butter and stir to incorporate. Taste the sauce and adjust the seasoning if necessary. Add the braised rabbit to the sauce and stir well.

WINE PAIRING **Viognier**

FOOD FOR THOUGHT *Serve this dish with Basil-Scented Potato Cakes (page 190) or Mashed Potatoes (page 191).*

Liberty Duck Breast with Capers, Olives, and Herb Pan Sauce

Serves 6

Liberty is the type of duck we cook with from Sonoma County Poultry. They are named for their free-range feeding and the company's humane breeding methods. Duck breasts are meaty, flavorful, and pan-sear perfectly. Don't fret if most of your capers end up in the pan; they will incorporate with the sauce. We have not added any extra salt to this recipe because the capers and the olives supply just enough.

- 6 duck breasts (8 to 10 ounces each) (chicken breasts or pork loin may be substituted)
- pepper
- ½ cup drained capers, pureed
- 2 tablespoons blended oil (page 7)
- 2 tablespoons minced shallots
- ½ cup approximately equal amounts pitted green and black olives
- 1 teaspoon minced garlic
- ½ tablespoon chopped fresh Italian parsley
- ½ tablespoon chopped fresh thyme
- ½ tablespoon chopped fresh sage
- ½ tablespoon chopped fresh marjoram
- 1 cup sherry
- 1 tablespoon unsalted butter

Preheat the oven to 375°F.

Trim the excess fat from the duck breasts and score the skin. Season the duck on both sides with pepper. Rub the pureed capers on the fatless side of the duck breasts.

In a large ovenproof pan, heat the oil over medium heat until very hot. Cook the duck breasts, fat side down, over medium heat for 5 minutes, until the fat starts to run. Remove the excess fat from the pan. Turn the duck breasts over and transfer the pan to the oven. Roast the duck for 8 minutes. Remove the duck breasts from the pan and let them rest for 5 minutes.

In the same pan cook the shallots, olives, garlic, and herbs over medium heat. Add the sherry. Stir and let the liquid reduce until slightly thick. Finish the sauce with the butter. Slice the duck breasts and spoon the sauce over the top.

Wine pairing **Mourvèdre**

Food for thought *Serve with Fingerling Potato Confit (page 189) or Roasted Potatoes (page 188).*

liberty ducks

Jim Reichardt, Petaluma, California

Jim seems like an ordinary guy. He is a nice, gentle man, and boy, what a worker! The last time I saw him, his delivery man was out sick and he was wheeling in our ducks himself. His ducks are literally the best I've ever tasted. When you serve duck confit every day, the product has to be the best.

Liberty Duck Breast with Orange Pomegranate Glaze

Serves 6

In this recipe the traditional French duck à l'orange has merged with pomegranates, a happy marriage. Sweet fruit sauces always complement the rich gamey flavor of the duck.

6 duck breasts (8 to 10 ounces each)
salt and pepper
2 tablespoons blended oil (page 7)
1 cup Orange Pomegranate Glaze (recipe follows)

Preheat the oven to 375°F.

Trim the excess fat from the duck breasts and score the skin. Season the duck on both sides with salt and pepper. In a large ovenproof pan, heat the oil over medium heat until very hot. Cook the duck breasts, fat side down, over medium heat for 5 minutes, until the fat starts to run. Remove the excess fat from the pan. Turn the duck breasts over and transfer the pan to the oven. Roast the duck for 8 minutes.

Remove the duck breasts from the pan and let them rest for 5 minutes before serving. Spoon the Orange Pomegranate Glaze over each duck breast.

Orange Pomegranate Glaze

Makes 1 cup

- ¼ cup chopped shallots
- 2 teaspoons blended oil (page 7)
- 1 teaspoon chopped fresh thyme
- zest of 1 lemon, grated
- zest of 2 oranges, grated
- 1 tablespoon sugar
- ¼ cup red wine vinegar
- 1 cup chicken stock (page 11)
- ½ cup light corn syrup
- 1 cup orange juice
- 3 cups pomegranate juice (available at health food stores)
- 1 tablespoon lemon juice
- 1 bay leaf
- 4 tablespoons (½ stick) unsalted butter, chilled and cut in pieces
- salt and pepper

Over medium heat, sauté the shallots in the oil in a heavy-bottomed saucepan until soft. Add the thyme, lemon zest, orange zest, and sugar. Reduce the heat and cook until the sugar begins to brown. Deglaze the pan with the red wine vinegar and reduce the liquid by half. Add the chicken stock, corn syrup, orange juice, pomegranate juice, lemon juice, and bay leaf and reduce to 1½ cups over medium heat. Strain the liquid to remove the solids and return to the pan. Whisk in the butter over low heat and season the sauce with salt and pepper.

Wine pairing Mourvèdre

Food for thought *Try these pan-seared duck breasts with the Dried Cherry and Green Peppercorn Sauce (page 166) or Tarragon-Mustard Sauce (page 127). On the side, serve with Roasted Potatoes (page 188), Fingerling Potato Confit (page 189), Mashed Potatoes (page 191), or Roasted Baby Beets and Figs (page 178).*

Duck Confit with Lentils, Applewood Smoked Bacon, and Cabbage

Serves 6

If I had to pick one last meal, I would start with the ripest assortment of figs with thinly sliced prosciutto, Lucque olives, extra virgin olive oil, and crusty French bread; a simple salad of mâche and baby arugula with a squeeze of lemon and grated Winchester Gouda; and this dish. I would finish with a plate of triple crème cheeses, fresh apricots, and probably a Snickers bar.

12 whole duck legs
½ cup kosher salt
15 garlic cloves, peeled
1 bunch fresh thyme
3 pounds rendered duck fat (see Sources, page 252)
2 tablespoons blended oil (page 7)

¼ pound applewood-smoked bacon, cut into small dice
½ onion, cut into small dice
½ celery stalk, cut into small dice
½ peeled carrot, cut into small dice
1 tablespoon minced garlic
1 pound French green lentils
2 bay leaves
1 tablespoon chopped fresh thyme
2 tablespoons chopped fresh Italian parsley sprigs
2 tablespoons Dijon mustard
5 cups chicken stock (page 11)
salt and pepper

Trim excess fat from the duck legs and reserve. Salt the duck well all over. Layer the duck legs in a large shallow pan with several cloves of garlic and thyme sprigs between each piece. Refrigerate for 24 hours.

To make the confit, preheat the oven to 325°F.

Put the rendered duck fat, reserved duck fat trimmings, and 1 cup water in a pot and slowly bring to a simmer. Simmer until the water evaporates and the fat has liquefied.

Rinse the salt from the duck and pat dry. Place the duck in a deep casserole dish and cover with the rendered fat. Cover the dish with foil and bake for about 3½ hours. (The duck is finished when the meat can easily be pulled from the bone.) Chill for at least 4 hours before searing.

Preheat the oven to 400°F.

Heat the oil in an ovenproof pan until hot. Sear the duck in the hot pan skin side down for 1 minute. Transfer the pan to the oven and cook the duck for 12 to 15 minutes, until the skin is crisp. Carefully remove the duck from the pan with a spatula, being careful not to tear the skin from the meat.

To make the lentils, in a large sauté pan, sauté the bacon over medium-high heat until crispy. Add the onion, celery, carrot, and garlic and cook until soft. Add the lentils, herbs, and mustard and stir. Add the chicken stock and bring to a boil. Reduce to a simmer. Cook until the lentils are tender, approximately 30 minutes, adding extra stock as needed. Season with salt and pepper. Serve the duck confit on a bed of lentils.

WINE PAIRING **Cinsault or Grenache**

FOOD FOR THOUGHT ***You can also serve duck confit with Mashed Potatoes (page 191) or Polenta Cakes (page 43). Make extra confit or save some for the Duck and Mushroom Rillettes (page 56), Duck Cassoulet (page 142), and White Bean and Duck Confit Soup (page 84).***

Duck Cassoulet

Serves 6

If there were one dish that truly speaks of rustic country-French cooking, it would be cassoulet. In France, cassoulet recipes vary from town to town. The selection of herbs and meats is different in each region, but the concept of a slow-cooked covered casserole remains the same. Don't be intimidated by the list of ingredients or the time it takes to make this dish; it will be well worth your effort. This is definitely a recipe to make for a group of friends. Cassoulet warms up any winter night and is often better the next day.

2 cups white beans soaked overnight in water to cover and drained
8 cups chicken stock (page 11)
3 tablespoons Pernod
2 bay leaves
4 garlic cloves, crushed
1 pound bacon, diced
2 pounds mild pork sausage links, cut into ½-inch pieces
2 carrots, peeled and cut into ½-inch dice
1 fennel bulb, cut into ½-inch dice
2 celery stalks, cut into ½-inch dice
¼ cup chopped fresh Italian parsley
2 tablespoons chopped fresh thyme
2 tablespoons chopped fresh sage
6 confited duck legs, meat removed from the bone and skin removed (page 140)
2 tablespoons unsalted butter
2 tablespoons fennel seeds
2 cups bread crumbs (preferably from French bread)

Preheat the oven to 350°F.

In a large saucepan, simmer the soaked beans in 7 cups of the chicken stock with the Pernod, bay leaves, and garlic for 1 hour or until the beans are soft.

Meanwhile, in a sauté pan, cook the bacon and sausage over high heat until browned, then remove. Sauté the carrots, fennel, celery, and fresh herbs in the bacon fat.

Combine the beans and duck with the bacon, sausage, and vegetable mixture in a large stainless steel bowl.

In a large pan, melt the butter with the fennel seeds and toss with the bread crumbs. Set aside.

Fill a large casserole dish with the cassoulet mixture, cover with the bread crumbs, and drizzle the remaining 1 cup chicken stock over the bread crumbs. Cover and bake for 1 hour.

Remove the cassoulet from the oven and remove the lid. Return to the oven and bake until the bread crumbs are golden brown, 5 to 8 minutes.

WINE PAIRING Grenache

FOOD FOR THOUGHT ***This cassoulet will be complete with a Simple Salad (page 88), and Roasted Asparagus (page 174).***

Braised Lamb Shanks

Serves 6

A slow oven braise allows the lamb to meld with the vegetables and the wine to create a luscious sauce. You cannot rush this dish; when cooked just right the lamb nearly falls off the bone.

6 lamb shanks, about 1 pound each
salt and pepper
½ cup flour
⅓ cup blended oil (page 7)
1 onion, roughly chopped
2 carrots, peeled and roughly chopped
1 fennel bulb, roughly chopped
6 garlic cloves
3 tablespoons chopped fresh thyme
3 tablespoons chopped fresh Italian parsley
½ cup tomato paste
1½ cups red wine
4 cups chicken stock (page 11)

Preheat the oven to 325°F.

Season the lamb shanks with salt and pepper and dredge in the flour.

In a large roasting pan, heat the oil over medium heat and sear the lamb shanks all over until golden. Remove the lamb to a bowl and set aside.

Put the onion, carrots, fennel, and garlic in the pan and cook over medium heat until they start to turn color and caramelize, 5 to 6 minutes. Add the thyme, parsley, and tomato paste and cook to soften the paste. Deglaze the pan with the red wine and add the chicken stock. Return the lamb to the roasting pan.

Bring the mixture to a simmer and cover with a lid. Braise in the oven for at least 2 hours or until the meat is tender and easily pulled from the bone, turning the lamb every half hour and skimming off the excess fat. Serve on a large platter.

Wine pairing Syrah

Food for thought *Lamb shanks are delicious with Mashed Potatoes (page 191) or Creamy Polenta (page 192).*

Lamb Medallions with Sonoma Mustard Sauce

Serves 6

Many people find autumn the most beautiful time in the vineyards, but the dry February and March days of the Sonoma mustard season challenge this thought. The vineyards are dotted with bright yellow mustard flowers that contrast with the dark vines, the first sign that spring is on its way. Our Sonoma Mustard Sauce uses French mustards but celebrates the Sonoma mustard season.

3 pounds lamb loin
salt and pepper
3 tablespoons herbes de Provence
2 tablespoons blended oil (page 7)
1½ cups Sonoma Mustard Sauce (recipe follows)

Preheat the oven to 350°F.

Rub the whole lamb loin with salt, pepper, and herbes de Provence. Heat the oil in an ovenproof skillet over high heat. Sear the lamb all over to retain the juices. Drain the excess oil.

Roast the lamb for about 10 minutes total for medium-rare to medium. Transfer the lamb to a platter and keep warm while you prepare the sauce. To serve, slice the lamb in ½-inch slices and spoon mustard sauce on top.

Sonoma Mustard Sauce

MAKES 2 CUPS

- 1½ tablespoons blended oil (page 7)
- 1 carrot, peeled and diced
- 1 medium onion, diced
- 3 sprigs fresh rosemary
- 1 celery stalk, diced
- 4 cups orange juice
- 1 cup white wine
- ¼ cup Dijon mustard
- ¼ cup whole-grain mustard
- 1 tablespoon honey
- 2 tablespoons heavy cream
- salt and pepper
- 2 tablespoons unsalted butter, at room temperature

Heat the oil in a medium saucepan over medium heat and sauté the carrot, onion, rosemary, and celery until tender. Add the orange juice and white wine and reduce by half. Add the mustards and honey and mix well. Add the cream, stir, and bring to a simmer. Strain the sauce and season with salt and pepper. Return the sauce to the heat and whisk in the butter.

WINE PAIRING Syrah

FOOD FOR THOUGHT *The lamb medallions taste great with Dried Cherry and Green Peppercorn Sauce (page 166), Tarragon-Mustard Sauce (page 127), Shallot and Red Wine Sauce (page 165), or Syrah Reduction Sauce (page 153). On the side, serve with Mashed Potatoes (page 191), Wild Mushroom Ragout (page 182), Creamy Polenta (page 192), or Roasted Baby Beets and Figs (page 178).*

Pan-Seared Calf's Liver with Cipollini Onions and Sherry Sauce

Serves 6

The first time I tasted calf's liver, I knew that it was one of my all-time favorite taste sensations. My first liver dish was a thick slab cooked medium-rare that oozed natural juices and was served with crunchy bacon. When I see guests grimace at the word liver, *I know they have never tasted the same liver dish that I did! Our version of "liver and onions" is enhanced by pancetta, sweet wild onions, and Spanish sherry. I like to serve this dish with mashed potatoes to sop up every last bit of sauce.*

5 tablespoons blended oil (page 7) or more if needed
¼ pound pancetta, chopped
3 tablespoons minced shallots
18 cipollini onions, blanched and peeled
1 tablespoon minced garlic
1 tablespoon chopped fresh thyme
¼ cup sherry (amontillado or manzanilla)
2 cups veal stock (page 13)
3 tablespoons unsalted butter
salt and pepper

1 cup flour
1 tablespoon salt
1 teaspoon pepper
3 pounds calf's liver, cut into 6 thin pieces

Preheat the oven to 400°F.

Heat 3 tablespoons of the oil in a large ovenproof sauté pan and cook the pancetta over medium heat until the fat is rendered. Add the shallots, onions, and garlic and cook until translucent; add the thyme. Deglaze the pan with the sherry and cook until the pan is dry. Add the veal stock and reduce by half. Add the butter to the reduced stock and season with salt and pepper. Set the sauce aside and keep warm.

In a dish, combine the flour, salt, and pepper and blend well. Heat the remaining 2 tablespoons oil in a large sauté pan. Be sure the pan is coated with the oil. Dredge the liver in the flour mixture and shake off any excess flour. Place the pieces of liver in the pan (do not crowd the pan) and brown on both sides, 3 minutes per side. Repeat until all the liver is browned, adding an additional tablespoon of oil if needed.

Place the browned liver on a baking sheet and bake for 2 to 3 minutes. Serve the liver on a large platter, smothered with the sauce.

WINE PAIRING Cinsault

Shape is a good part of the fig's delight.

JANE GRIGSON

Pan-Seared Beef Fillet with Tarragon Butter

Serves 6

This is a melt-in-your-mouth fillet that really doesn't need any sauce, but the simple tarragon butter melts with the natural juices of the beef to create a simple sauce. Generously season your fillets; the salt and pepper add a punch of flavor during the searing process.

6 beef fillets (6 to 8 ounces each)
1 tablespoon olive oil
salt and pepper
½ pound Tarragon Butter (recipe follows)

Preheat the oven to 400°F.

Rub the fillets all over with ½ tablespoon of the olive oil; season generously with salt and pepper. In an ovenproof pan over medium-high heat, heat the remaining ½ tablespoon olive oil and sear the fillets all over. Roast for 7 minutes. Let rest for 5 minutes before serving, then dollop a spoonful of tarragon butter on each fillet.

Tarragon Butter

Makes ½ pound

1 teaspoon blended oil (page 7)
1 tablespoon minced shallots
½ cup white wine
¼ cup minced fresh tarragon
½ pound (2 sticks) unsalted butter, at room temperature
2 teaspoons lemon juice
salt

In a saucepan, heat the oil over medium heat and cook the shallots until translucent, 3 to 4 minutes. Add the white wine and tarragon. Reduce the liquid to 2 tablespoons and cool.

In a food processor, whip the butter and add the tarragon mixture, lemon juice, and salt to taste.

Mound the butter on a sheet of plastic wrap and roll into a log 1½ inches in diameter. Refrigerate or freeze until needed.

Wine pairing **Mourvèdre**

Food for thought *Serve these delicious fillets with the Shallot and Red Wine Sauce (page 165), or the Syrah Reduction Sauce (page 153). On the side, serve with Roasted Potatoes (page 188), Red Chard, Cheddar, and Potato Gratin (page 187), Wild Mushroom Ragout (page 182), or Balsamic Shallots (page 172).*

Hazelnut-and-Peppercorn-Crusted Beef Tenderloin with Syrah Reduction Sauce

Serves 6

After refrigeration, this crust will cook into the tenderloin and give it a crunchy texture. When preparing the reduction sauce, let the ingredients reduce slowly to intensify the flavors.

2 tablespoons chopped hazelnuts, toasted
2 tablespoons black peppercorns
2½ pounds beef tenderloin or 6 fillets
salt
2 tablespoons extra virgin olive oil
Syrah Reduction Sauce (recipe follows)

Mix the chopped hazelnuts and the peppercorns together in a bowl. Rub the whole tenderloin with the mixture, pressing it gently into the beef. Generously season with salt. Refrigerate, covered, for at least 4 hours or overnight.

Preheat the oven to 375°F.

Heat the olive oil in an ovenproof skillet over high heat. Sear the beef all over to retain its juices. Place the beef in the oven for about 15 minutes, or until the internal temperature reaches 150°F on an instant-read thermometer for medium. (Cook 5 minutes less for rare meat.)

Transfer the beef to a platter to rest for about 10 minutes. Keep warm while you prepare the sauce.

Syrah Reduction Sauce

Makes 1 cup

- 1 onion, cut into small dice
- 1 celery stalk, cut into small dice
- 1 carrot, peeled and cut into small dice
- 1 leek, cut into small dice
- 1 Roma tomato, chopped
- 2 garlic cloves, crushed
- 2 cups Syrah (any dry, full-bodied red wine may be substituted)
- 4 cups veal stock (page 13)
- bouquet garni (3 thyme sprigs, 3 to 4 Italian parsley sprigs, ½ teaspoon black peppercorns, 1 bay leaf)
- ½ teaspoon unsweetened cocoa powder
- salt and pepper

Sauté the onion, celery, carrot, leek, tomato, and garlic over medium heat in a saucepan until lightly browned. Deglaze the pan with the Syrah and reduce the liquid to 1 cup. Add the veal stock, bouquet garni, and cocoa powder and slowly reduce the liquid by half, skimming constantly. Strain the sauce and adjust the seasoning.

Wine pairing Syrah

Food for thought *Serve with Haricots Verts (page 173), Roasted Asparagus (page 174), or Basil-Scented Potato Cakes (page 190).*

Braised Beef Short Ribs

Serves 6

Every week in winter we offer different plats du jour, including these short ribs, which sell out every time. These are rich, fall-off-the-bone, stick-to-the-ribs short ribs. Ask your butcher for six 2 by 3-inch rib portions; he will know what to do.

Marinade

3 tablespoons minced garlic
1 tablespoon salt
1 tablespoon pepper
1 tablespoon chopped fresh Italian parsley
1 tablespoon chopped fresh thyme
1½ cups red wine
½ cup extra virgin olive oil
1 tablespoon sherry vinegar

Braise

6 short ribs (2 by 3-inch ribs)
salt and pepper
2 tablespoons blended oil (page 7)
1 carrot, peeled and cut into ½-inch dice
2 medium onions, cut into ½-inch dice
3 celery stalks, cut into ½-inch dice
3 Roma tomatoes, roughly chopped
10 cups veal stock (page 13)
bouquet garni (3 thyme sprigs, 3 to 4 Italian parsley sprigs, ½ teaspoon black peppercorns, 1 bay leaf)

In a bowl, make the marinade by mixing together the garlic, salt, pepper, herbs, ½ cup of the red wine, the olive oil, and sherry vinegar. Pour the marinade over the ribs and marinate for at least 12 hours.

Preheat a grill. Scrape the excess marinade off the ribs and season with salt and pepper. Sear the ribs all over on the grill. Set the ribs aside.

Heat the oil in a large roasting pan. Add the carrot, onions, and celery and cook over medium heat until the vegetables are caramelized, about 3 to 4 minutes. Add the tomatoes and cook for 5 minutes. Deglaze the pan with 1 cup red wine. Add the veal stock, bouquet garni, and ribs and bring to a simmer. Cover the pan and roast for 4 hours, turning the ribs every half hour and removing excess fat. Remove the ribs, smother with the sauce, and serve.

Wine pairing **Syrah**

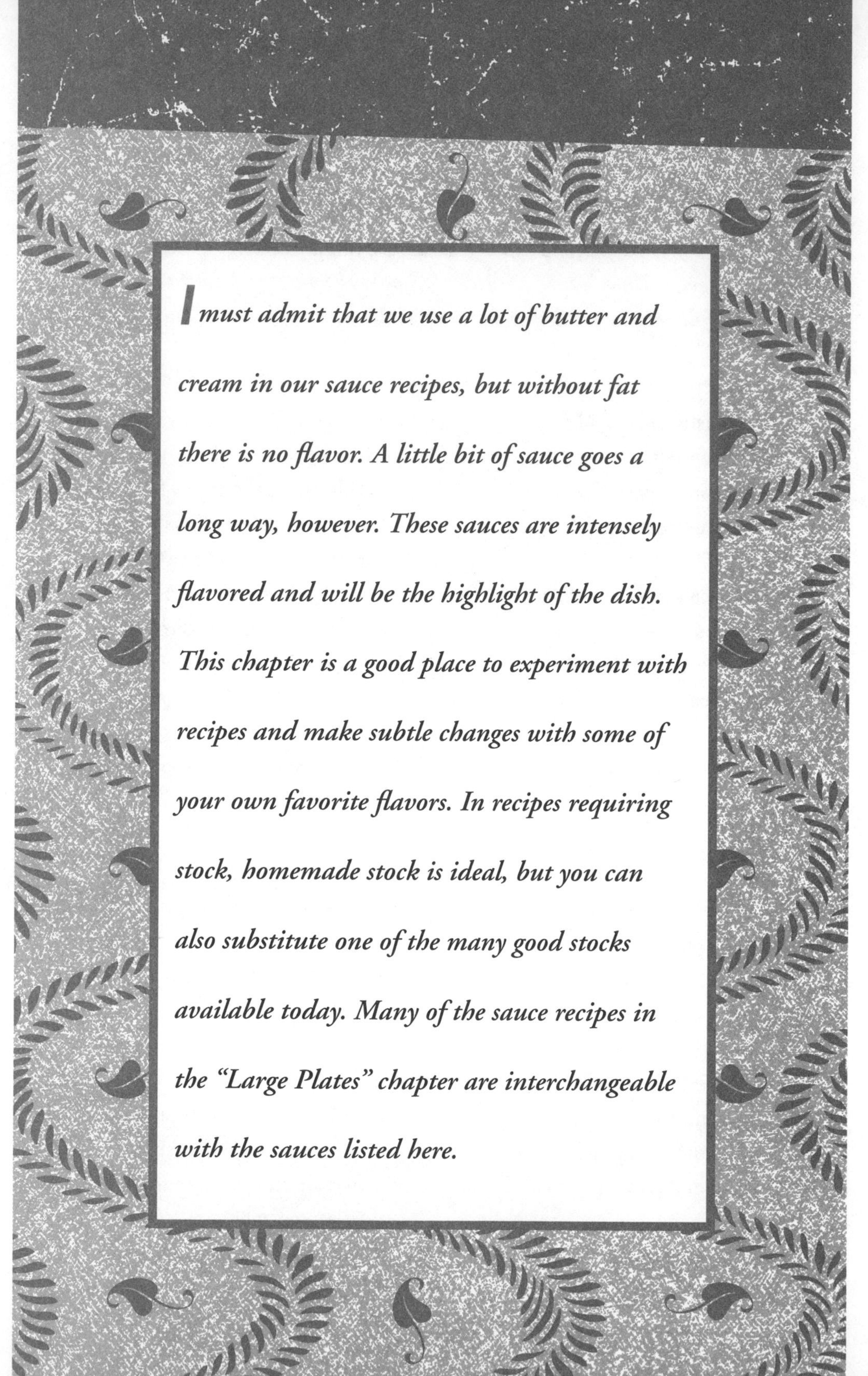

I must admit that we use a lot of butter and cream in our sauce recipes, but without fat there is no flavor. A little bit of sauce goes a long way, however. These sauces are intensely flavored and will be the highlight of the dish. This chapter is a good place to experiment with recipes and make subtle changes with some of your own favorite flavors. In recipes requiring stock, homemade stock is ideal, but you can also substitute one of the many good stocks available today. Many of the sauce recipes in the "Large Plates" chapter are interchangeable with the sauces listed here.

sauce over and under

Saffron Butter
Basil Aïoli
Caper Aïoli
Roasted Garlic Aïoli
Tarragon Aïoli
Celery Root Remoulade
Fig and Olive Relish
Pistou
Red Pepper Rouille
Warm Chive Vinaigrette
Saffron Balsamic Essence
Blood Orange Sauce
Roasted Tomato and Garlic Sauce
Shallot and Red Wine Sauce
Citrus Beurre Blanc
Dried Cherry and Green Peppercorn Sauce
Tomato Cream Sauce
Saffron Cream Sauce
Sorrel Sauce

Saffron Butter

Makes ½ pound

1 teaspoon blended oil (page 7)
1 tablespoon minced shallots
½ cup white wine
1 teaspoon saffron threads
½ pound (2 sticks) unsalted butter, at room temperature
2 teaspoons lemon juice
salt

In a saucepan, heat the oil over medium heat and cook the shallots until translucent. Add the white wine and saffron. Reduce the liquid to 2 tablespoons and let cool.

In a food processor, whip the butter and add the saffron mixture, lemon juice, and salt to taste. Mound the butter on a sheet of plastic wrap and roll into a log 1½ inches in diameter. Refrigerate or freeze until needed.

Basil Aïoli

Makes 1 cup

3 egg yolks
1 teaspoon minced garlic
3 tablespoons chopped fresh basil, blanched
4 teaspoons lemon juice
1 teaspoon Champagne vinegar
¾ cup blended oil (page 7)
salt and pepper

Combine the egg yolks, garlic, basil, lemon juice, and vinegar in a food processor. Pulse to blend the ingredients and slowly add the oil. Season with salt and pepper to taste. The aïoli will keep for 7 days in the refrigerator.

Caper Aïoli

MAKES 1 CUP

3 egg yolks
1 teaspoon minced garlic
3 tablespoons capers, drained
4 teaspoons lemon juice
1 teaspoon Champagne vinegar
¾ cup blended oil (page 7)
salt and pepper

Combine the egg yolks, garlic, capers, lemon juice, and vinegar in a food processor. Pulse to blend the ingredients and slowly add the oil. Season with salt and pepper to taste. The aïoli will keep for 7 days in the refrigerator.

Roasted Garlic Aïoli

MAKES 1 CUP

1 cup blended oil (page 7)
10 garlic cloves, peeled and sliced in half, plus ¼ teaspoon minced garlic
3 egg yolks
1 tablespoon lemon juice
salt and pepper

Heat the oil in a saucepan and cook the garlic cloves over medium heat, allowing them to brown lightly. Reduce the heat and cook the garlic over very low heat until soft, about 7 minutes. Remove the pan from the heat and strain the garlic, reserving the oil. Let the oil cool.

In a food processor, combine the egg yolks, lemon juice, minced garlic, and cooked garlic. Slowly add the cooled garlic oil to form an emulsion. Season with salt and pepper to taste. The aïoli will keep for 7 days in the refrigerator.

Tarragon Aïoli

Makes 1 cup

3 egg yolks
1 teaspoon minced garlic
3 tablespoons chopped fresh tarragon
4 teaspoons lemon juice
1 teaspoon Champagne vinegar
¾ cup blended oil (page 7)
salt and pepper

Combine the egg yolks, garlic, tarragon, lemon juice, and vinegar in a food processor. Pulse to blend the ingredients and slowly add the oil. Season with salt and pepper to taste. The aïoli will keep for 7 days in the refrigerator.

Celery Root Remoulade

Makes 1½ cups

1 cup Caper Vinaigrette (page 117)
1 tablespoon chopped fresh chervil
2 tablespoons chopped fresh Italian parsley
1 tablespoon chopped cornichons
½ teaspoon Worcestershire sauce
dash of Tabasco
¼ teaspoon paprika
¼ cup grated celery root (see Note)
salt and pepper

Combine all the ingredients in a bowl, adding salt and pepper to taste. The remoulade will keep for 3 to 4 days in the refrigerator.

Note: Celery root is available in the produce section of most markets.

Fig and Olive Relish

Makes 4 cups

¼ cup olive oil
1 tablespoon minced shallots
2 cups dried figs, quartered
1 tablespoon mustard seeds
½ cup sugar
1 cup Fig Balsamic Vinegar (see page 249)
2 tablespoons whole-grain mustard
pinch of black pepper
1 cup chopped pitted mixed olives

In a medium saucepan, heat the olive oil and sauté the shallots over medium heat until translucent, 1 to 2 minutes. Add the dried figs, mustard seeds, sugar, fig balsamic vinegar, mustard, and pepper. Reduce the heat and simmer until the figs are soft and the compote has thickened to the consistency of preserves, about 10 minutes. Mix in the olives and cool. The relish will keep for 14 days in the refrigerator.

Pistou

Makes 1¼ cups

3 large tomatoes
1 cup fresh basil leaves, packed
1 tablespoon minced garlic
½ cup extra virgin olive oil
⅓ cup grated hard cheese
salt and pepper

In a pot of boiling water, blanch the tomatoes for 30 seconds to loosen the skins. Plunge the tomatoes in ice water and drain. Remove the tomato skins and dice the flesh and remove the seeds.

In a blender, puree the basil, garlic, and olive oil. Pour into a bowl and add the tomatoes and grated cheese. Stir well. Season with salt and pepper to taste. The pistou will keep for 5 days in the refrigerator.

Red Pepper Rouille

MAKES 1½ CUPS

2 red bell peppers
¼ teaspoon cayenne
1 tablespoon lemon juice
1 egg yolk
1 teaspoon minced garlic
1 cup blended oil (page 7)
salt and white pepper

Roast the peppers all over on a grill or under a broiler until the skin is well charred. Place them in a container, cover with plastic wrap, and refrigerate until cool. Peel and seed the peppers.

In a food processor, puree the peppers with the cayenne, lemon juice, egg yolk, and garlic. Slowly add the oil to create an emulsion; season with salt and pepper to taste. The rouille will keep for 7 days in the refrigerator.

Warm Chive Vinaigrette

MAKES 1 CUP

1 tablespoon minced shallots
2 tablespoons honey
2 tablespoons Dijon mustard
½ cup Champagne vinegar
1 tablespoon plus ½ cup blended oil (page 7)
salt and pepper
1 bunch chives, minced

Sauté the shallots in 1 tablespoon oil over high heat in a sauté pan until soft. Add the honey and mustard and mix together with a whisk. Deglaze the pan with the vinegar and then remove from the heat. Slowly whisk in the remaining ½ cup oil. Season with salt and pepper to taste and add the chives. Serve immediately.

Saffron Balsamic Essence

MAKES ¾ CUP

1 tablespoon blended oil (page 7)
3 tablespoons minced shallots
pinch of saffron threads
1 cup white wine
1 cup balsamic vinegar
1 bay leaf
1 teaspoon black peppercorns
1½ cups chicken stock (page 11)
¼ pound (1 stick) unsalted butter, at room temperature
salt and pepper

Heat the oil in a saucepan and sauté the shallots with the saffron until translucent. Deglaze the pan with the white wine and reduce the liquid to several tablespoons. Add the vinegar, bay leaf, and peppercorns and reduce the liquid by half. Add the chicken stock and reduce again by half. Strain the sauce through cheesecloth and skim any fat or oil off the surface. Allow to cool slightly, then place the sauce in a blender and blend with the butter. Season with salt and pepper to taste.

Blood Orange Sauce

MAKES 1 CUP

- 1½ cups blood orange juice (from 7 to 8 oranges)
- 2 cups orange juice
- ¼ cup grenadine
- ½ star anise

Combine all the ingredients in a small saucepan and reduce the liquid to 1 cup over medium heat. Strain and cool. The sauce will keep for 10 days in the refrigerator.

Roasted Tomato and Garlic Sauce

MAKES 3 CUPS

2 pounds tomatoes, stem ends cored
12 garlic cloves, crushed
2 tablespoons balsamic vinegar
¼ cup extra virgin olive oil
1½ teaspoons salt
¼ teaspoon white pepper

Preheat the oven to 450°F.

Quarter the tomatoes. In a large bowl, mix the remaining ingredients together with the tomatoes, then spread the tomatoes out on a large baking sheet and roast for 20 minutes or until soft. Put the tomatoes in a blender and process until smooth; adjust the seasoning. The sauce will keep for 5 days in the refrigerator.

Shallot and Red Wine Sauce

MAKES 1½ CUPS

1 tablespoon blended oil (page 7)
1 cup quartered shallots
1 tablespoon minced garlic
1 tablespoon chopped fresh thyme
1 tablespoon flour
¼ cup brandy
1½ cups red wine
2½ cups veal stock (page 13; chicken stock may be substituted)
2 tablespoons unsalted butter
salt and pepper

Heat the oil in a deep sauté pan and caramelize the shallots. Add the garlic and cook until it begins to brown. Add the thyme and stir to incorporate; add the flour and mix well. Deglaze the pan with the brandy. Allow the alcohol to burn off and then add the red wine. Reduce the liquid by two-thirds, add the stock, and reduce again by two-thirds. Remove the pan from the heat and whisk in the butter. Season with salt and pepper to taste. The sauce will keep for 5 days in the refrigerator.

Citrus Beurre Blanc

Makes 1⅓ cups

- ¼ cup white wine
- 1 tablespoon minced shallots
- zest of 1 orange, finely chopped
- zest of 1 lemon, finely chopped
- 2 tablespoons lemon juice
- ½ cup heavy cream
- ½ pound (2 sticks) unsalted butter, room temperature, cut into pieces
- salt and pepper

In a saucepan, combine the wine, shallots, orange and lemon zest, and lemon juice over medium heat. Reduce the liquid until the pan is almost dry. Add the cream and reduce by half. Reduce the heat to low and slowly whisk in the butter. Season with salt and pepper to taste. The sauce will keep for 5 days in the refrigerator.

Dried Cherry and Green Peppercorn Sauce

Makes 1¾ cups

- 3 tablespoons unsalted butter
- ¼ cup minced shallots
- 1 teaspoon green peppercorns, drained
- 3 tablespoons tomato paste
- 2 tablespoons chopped fresh rosemary
- 1 cup dried cherries
- ¼ cup brandy
- ½ cup port
- 3 cups chicken stock (page 11)
- salt and pepper

Melt 1 tablespoon of the butter in a saucepan until just browned. Add the shallots and peppercorns and sauté until the shallots are soft. Add the tomato paste, rosemary, and dried cherries. Cook until the tomato paste begins to stick to the bottom of the pan. Deglaze the pan with the brandy and port. Reduce for 5 minutes over medium heat. Add the chicken stock and reduce the liquid to 1½ cups. Whisk in the remaining 2 tablespoons butter and season with salt and pepper to taste. The sauce will keep for 5 days in the refrigerator.

Tomato Cream Sauce

MAKES 1 CUP

1 pound tomatoes, cut in half (the riper the tomato, the better the flavor of the sauce)
2 tablespoons minced garlic
1 tablespoon balsamic vinegar
1 tablespoon blended oil (page 7)
salt and pepper
¼ cup heavy cream
2 tablespoons olive oil

Preheat the oven to 375°F.

In a stainless steel bowl, toss the tomatoes with the garlic, vinegar, and oil and season with salt and pepper to taste. Spread the tomatoes out on a baking sheet and roast for 30 minutes. Let cool. Puree the tomatoes, cream, and olive oil in a food processor. Strain the sauce and adjust the seasoning. (If the sauce needs to be reheated before serving and seems too thick, thin it with warm water or chicken stock.) This sauce will keep for 5 days in the refrigerator.

I love long life better than figs.

SHAKESPEARE

Saffron Cream Sauce

Makes 1 cup

1 teaspoon blended oil (page 7)
1 tablespoon minced shallots
½ cup white wine
pinch of saffron threads
1½ cups heavy cream
salt and white pepper

Heat the oil in a sauté pan over medium heat, add the shallots, and cook until soft. Add the white wine and saffron and reduce the liquid by half. Add the cream and reduce the liquid to 1 cup. Season with salt and white pepper to taste. The sauce will keep for 5 days in the refrigerator.

Sorrel Sauce

Makes 1¾ cups

- 1 cup packed sorrel leaves (about 1 bunch)
- ¼ cup packed spinach
- 1 tablespoon blended oil (page 7)
- 1 tablespoon minced shallots
- 1 teaspoon black peppercorns
- 1 bay leaf
- ½ cup white wine
- ¾ cup heavy cream
- ½ pound (2 sticks) unsalted butter, chilled and cut into 8 pieces
- salt and white pepper

Puree the sorrel and spinach in a blender with ¾ cup water and set aside. Heat the oil in a saucepan and gently sauté the shallots until translucent. Add the peppercorns and bay leaf and deglaze the pan with the white wine. Reduce the wine until the pan is dry, add the cream, and reduce by one-third. Whisk in the butter one piece at a time over low heat until incorporated. Strain the cream mixture into a bowl and add the sorrel puree. Season with salt and pepper to taste. The sauce will keep for 5 days in the refrigerator.

There is a lot of versatility in the following recipes. They work well with many of the dishes in the "Large Plates" chapter, and some work nicely on their own. Sometimes the side dishes are better than the main course!

on the side

Balsamic Shallots
Balsamic Onions
Haricots Verts
Roasted Asparagus
Roasted Cauliflower
Wilted Greens
Roasted Baby Beets and Figs
Orange-Scented Braised Endive
Braised Leeks
Wild Mushroom Ragout
Apple-Yam Gratin
Red Chard, Cheddar, and Potato Gratin
Roasted Potatoes
Fingerling Potato Confit
Basil-Scented Potato Cakes
Mashed Potatoes
Creamy Polenta
Risotto Cakes
Citrus Pearl Couscous
Pearl Couscous and French Olives

Balsamic Shallots

Makes 3/4 cup

These shallots have a strong flavor and are a nice accompaniment for charcuterie platters and beef and pork dishes.

1 tablespoon blended oil (see page 7)
1 pound shallots, halved
1 teaspoon chopped fresh thyme
½ cup honey
1 cup balsamic vinegar
salt and pepper

Heat the oil in a large sauté pan and sauté the shallots until lightly browned, about 10 minutes. Add the thyme and cook for a minute more. Add the honey and then the vinegar. Cook the mixture until the shallots are soft and the vinegar has been reduced by three-quarters. Season with salt and pepper to taste.

Balsamic Onions

Makes 1 cup

These onions are terrific with pâté or terrines. They are also a great topping for our pissaladière (page 49) or served simply on grilled bread with goat cheese.

1 tablespoon blended oil (page 7)
4 medium onions, sliced
1 teaspoon chopped fresh thyme
1 teaspoon minced garlic
½ cup honey
1 cup balsamic vinegar
salt and pepper

Heat the oil in a large sauté pan and sauté the onions until lightly browned. Add the thyme and garlic and cook for a minute until the ingredients are blended. Add the honey and then the vinegar. Cook until the onions are well done and the vinegar is reduced by three-quarters. Season with salt and pepper to taste.

Haricots Verts

Serves 6

Haricots verts is the French name for green beans. These delicate slender beans cook quickly and are a staple in the restaurant. For many of our side dishes we blanch our vegetables briefly and place them in an ice bath for 30 seconds to a minute to maintain their texture and set their color before reheating.

2 tablespoons extra virgin olive oil
1 teaspoon minced garlic
1 tablespoon minced shallots
2 teaspoons chopped fresh Italian parsley
2 teaspoons chopped fresh sage
¾ pound haricots verts, stemmed and blanched (green or yellow wax beans may be substituted)
salt and pepper

In a sauté pan large enough to hold all the beans, heat the olive oil over medium heat and sauté the garlic and shallots until soft. Add the herbs. Add the haricots verts, toss to coat with the herbs and oil, and heat until hot, about 2 minutes. Season with salt and pepper to taste.

Roasted Asparagus

Serves 6

Asparagus are often blanched and sautéed, but I prefer mine roasted. This is a simple method that does not require a lot of attention while you prepare the other dishes on your menu. For a delectable variation, add some crushed garlic cloves or baby leeks to the asparagus before roasting.

36 asparagus spears, bottom stalks trimmed and peeled
3 tablespoons olive oil
salt and pepper

Preheat the oven to 400°F.

Place the asparagus spears in a single layer on a baking sheet. Drizzle with the olive oil, making sure each spear is lightly coated with oil. Season the spears with salt and pepper and roast in the oven for 15 minutes or until tender.

A small garden, figs, a little cheese, and, along with this, three or four good friends—such was luxury to Epicurus.

NIETZSCHE

Roasted Cauliflower

SERVES 6

Even if you hate cauliflower, you'll love this recipe. You will have an earthy side dish that complements chicken, pork, or beef entrees. Make sure that you coat the cauliflower well with olive oil before roasting. You can substitute broccoli with equally delicious results.

1 medium cauliflower, broken into medium florets
2 tablespoons extra virgin olive oil
pinch of kosher salt
¼ cup bread crumbs
4 tablespoons (½ stick) unsalted butter
1 tablespoon minced shallots
½ teaspoon chopped fresh thyme
1 tablespoon chopped fresh Italian parsley
½ tablespoon chopped fresh rosemary
½ teaspoon sherry vinegar
1 teaspoon whole-grain mustard
cracked pepper

Preheat the oven to 450°F.

In a heavy-bottomed pan, toss the cauliflower with the olive oil and salt. Roast the cauliflower for 15 minutes and test for doneness or desired texture. When the cauliflower is done, toss with the bread crumbs and set aside.

Immediately heat the butter in a sauté pan and sauté the shallots, thyme, parsley, and rosemary. Let the butter melt and brown slightly. Stir in the sherry vinegar and whole-grain mustard. Return the cauliflower to the sauté pan and toss well to coat. Season with salt and cracked pepper to taste.

Wilted Greens

SERVES 6

I love sautéed greens just about any time of the year, lightly coated with olive oil and garlic. There are such wonderful types of greens available today, it's almost impossible to choose just one. Add some mustard greens, leftover beet greens, and baby spinach to your mix for a rainbow of flavors.

2 pounds greens, such as chard or kale, stemmed and well cleaned
2 tablespoons olive oil
1 tablespoon minced garlic
2 tablespoons minced shallots
¼ cup white wine
1 tablespoon unsalted butter
salt and pepper

Tear the greens into large pieces. Heat the olive oil in a large pan and sauté the garlic and shallots. Add the greens and then add the white wine. Cover. Cook until tender, stirring so as not to burn the bottom, 4 to 5 minutes. Add the butter and season with salt and pepper to taste.

Roasted Baby Beets and Figs

Serves 6

You won't see this combination on too many menus. This was a special recipe we designed specifically for the annual Fig Festival in Santa Monica, California. We served it with a rack of lamb and chard-potato gratin. All these flavors were excellent together and went nicely with the Rhône varietals they were paired with.

36 to 40 baby beets (such as Chioggia, Golden, or red)
12 mixed figs, stems removed, halved
salt and pepper
1 tablespoon unsalted butter

Preheat the oven to 350°F.

Remove the tops and bottoms of the beets, cutting the beets down to where you can just begin to see the flesh. (Save the beet tops for the sautéed greens you can serve as another side dish.) Scrub the beets gently under running water to remove any dirt or grit.

Place the beets in a deep baking dish. Fill the dish with water until the beets are halfway submerged. (Be sure to cook beet varieties separately to preserve their color.) Cover with foil and roast until the beets are soft, about 1½ hours. Test the beets by poking with a toothpick. Remove the pan from the oven and allow the beets to cool. Rub the skin off with your hands and trim away any blemishes that remain. Cut the beets in half and set aside and keep warm.

Season the figs with salt and pepper. Melt the butter over medium heat in a sauté pan and place the figs facedown in the pan until lightly browned. Remove the figs from the pan. Toss the figs and beets together and adjust the seasoning.

beets

Beets are very simple to prepare and perfect for a winter salad or roasted and served as a side dish. When we cook beets for our beet salad, we separate the varietals because they are very messy to clean and the beet juices can easily run together. Save the greens and use them in the Wilted Greens recipe (page 177).

CHIOGGIA beets are also known as striped beets, and they are fantastic looking, with a concentric red-and-white-ringed flesh. These beets date back to the 1840s. They have a sweet peppery flavor.

GOLDEN beets have an orange-pink skin with golden flesh. They are tender and mild with a sweet taste.

RED beets are the most popular beets on the market. They are a dark, deep red in color with a juicy, earthy flavor.

Orange-Scented Braised Endive

Serves 6

Endive, most often found in salads, is an excellent vegetable to braise. The leaves stay firmly together and the slow cooking brings out its best flavors. You can use either Belgian endive or the red-flecked variety. Both complement the citrus and herb combination of this recipe.

6 heads endive
2 tablespoons unsalted butter
1 teaspoon minced garlic
1 tablespoon honey
2 cups orange juice
½ teaspoon fresh Italian parsley
½ teaspoon fresh thyme
salt and pepper

Cut the endives in half. Melt the butter in a sauté pan and sauté the endive until slightly caramelized, 2 to 3 minutes. Add the garlic, honey, orange juice, parsley, and thyme and cook until the endive is tender, 15 to 20 minutes. Season with salt and pepper to taste.

Braised Leeks

SERVES 6

When you trim down the leeks, there will be nothing to keep them together during the braising process, so don't be alarmed if they don't stay together. Braising leeks tenderizes their tough fibers, so take your time and cook them slowly. As leeks mature they often hold a bit of dirt between their leaves, so make sure you wash them well.

12 leeks, trimmed
2 tablespoons unsalted butter
1 teaspoon minced garlic
1 teaspoon chopped fresh Italian parsley
1 teaspoon chopped fresh thyme
½ cup white wine
2 cups chicken stock (page 11)
salt and pepper
crisp pancetta or prosciutto

Split the leeks in half and place in a bowl of water to remove any sand or grit. Remove from the water and pat dry.

In a large sauté pan, melt the butter and add the leeks flat side down. Sauté until slightly browned, then turn the leeks over. After the leeks have browned slightly on both sides, add the garlic and herbs and cook for an additional 5 minutes over medium-low heat. Deglaze the pan with the wine and allow the liquid to simmer until the pan is almost completely dry. Add the stock and simmer until the pan is almost dry. (The leeks should be soft and tender enough to cut with a fork.) Season with salt and pepper and sprinkle crispy pancetta or prosciutto on top of the leeks before serving.

Wild Mushroom Ragout

Serves 6

This is one of my all-time favorite recipes from our kitchen. As a kid I remember only one type of mushroom—the button mushroom. But today there are many different types of mushrooms available at the market. They come in all shapes, colors, and sizes. We are lucky to have Stephen bring his foraged mushrooms to the restaurant, freshly picked just hours before being cooked. The woody, earthy flavors of mushrooms are intensified by being sautéed, and the herbs and garlic add another layer of flavor.

¼ cup extra virgin olive oil
½ cup minced pancetta
4 cups assorted wild mushrooms, such as chanterelle, shiitake, oyster, and cremini, cleaned and sliced
1 tablespoon chopped fresh thyme
1 tablespoon chopped fresh sage
1 tablespoon chopped fresh Italian parsley
1 tablespoon chopped fresh tarragon
2 garlic cloves, minced
salt and pepper
½ cup red wine
3 tablespoons unsalted butter

Heat the olive oil in a large heavy-bottomed skillet and sauté the pancetta over low heat until golden brown. Add the mushrooms, herbs, and garlic and cook until golden brown. Season with salt and pepper to taste. Deglaze the pan with the red wine and reduce the liquid by half. Remove from the heat and stir in the butter.

Food for thought *Serve the mushroom ragout over one of your favorite creamy cheeses; Cambozola, Camembert, or Roquefort work well. Serve pieces of crusty French bread on the side to soak up all the juices. The ragout is also a wonderful accompaniment to Lamb Medallions with Sonoma Mustard Sauce (page 146), Grilled Chicken Breasts with Tarragon-Mustard Sauce (page 126), and Grilled Pork Chops with Apple Cider Sauce (page 132).*

the forager's bounty

Today many different types of mushrooms are available year-round in markets, allowing us to use mushrooms in many of our recipes. They each have their own distinct flavor and add a unique essence to the recipe they are used in. The following mushrooms come from Stephen, our forager, or through produce companies.

BLACK TRUMPETS or **BLACK CHANTERELLES** are foraged primarily in northern California. The season is from late summer to late autumn. These mushrooms are hollow but very versatile in cooking; the flavor shines through during braising or prolonged cooking. Black trumpet mushrooms are a delicious accompaniment to duck and other game.

BLUE OYSTERS add a velvety texture to any recipe that includes mushrooms. These mushrooms are delicate and juicy and their slightly salty flavor is excellent with fish or poultry dishes.

CREMINI are similar to button mushrooms but have a light tan to rich brown color. They have a dense and earthy flavor and are extremely easy to work with.

CHANTERELLES are the best-known wild mushrooms on the West Coast. They are the highlight of the wild mushroom season, which runs from June through November. These lovely, yellow-orange mushrooms are dainty and delicate and have a fruity fragrance and chewy texture. They are abundant in the oak woodlands of California during the winter. When they are available we use them in our Pan-Roasted Monkfish (page 119) and our Wild Mushroom Risotto (page 110).

CINNAMON CAPS have a slightly crunchy texture and a mild, earthy flavor. They are unusual in color and their interesting appearance enhances the visual appeal of any dish. The flavor of these mushrooms complements meat and poultry. Cinnamon caps maintain their density during cooking and add texture to sauces and risottos.

HEDGEHOGS are similar to chanterelles in color and texture but have a layer of soft spines on the underside of the cap instead of ridges. They are foraged from late summer to midwinter.

LOBSTERS are hearty with a dense texture and a bright reddish-orange color. These are very meaty and rich in flavor. These mushrooms are available in the summer through fall.

MORELS are just about the most exciting part of spring. Morels are plentiful mid-April through mid-June but can be obtained from Mexico at a higher price during the fall and winter. Their hollow, honeycombed caps are distinctive but blend in easily with their surroundings. Morel mushrooms must always be cooked before eating—never, ever eat them raw. The easiest way to clean this type of mushroom is to slice each one in half to make sure there is nothing hiding inside, like a worm, and then gently rinse in a light stream of water and pat dry. Do not soak these mushrooms in water. The flavor intensity of the morel is second only to a truffle.

PORCINI are regarded as the great reward of mushroom hunting. They have a wonderful nutty flavor and are extremely versatile. Porcini mushrooms can grow very big and generally weigh more than two pounds. The porcini season is from spring to fall.

PORTOBELLOS are fantastic grilled. These mushrooms have a dense texture and a rich, earthy, meaty flavor.

SHIITAKES are very versatile. They can be sautéed, broiled, grilled, or sliced thin and tossed in pastas and risottos. Their meaty flavor enhances almost any dish. This dark brown mushroom has an earthy fragrance and full-bodied texture. The shiitake stems create deeply flavored mushroom stocks.

YELLOW FOOTS can be found in California from winter to spring. They are excellent for cooking and work well in any recipe that calls for chanterelle mushrooms.

Apple-Yam Gratin

Serves 12

This gratin requires a bit of time and effort to prepare, but it's more than worth it. Be sure to sprinkle the layers liberally with cheese.

3 Fuji apples, peeled and cored
1 yam, peeled
6 russet potatoes, peeled
2 cups heavy cream
½ teaspoon minced garlic
1 teaspoon chopped fresh thyme
1 pound Cheddar, grated (preferably Joe Matos's St. George; see Sources, page 251)
salt and white pepper
¼ pound prosciutto, very thinly sliced

nonstick cooking spray

Preheat the oven to 350°F.

Cut the apples and yam into ⅛-inch-thick slices and slice the potatoes to a 1/16-inch thickness with a mandoline. In a small pan, over medium heat, heat the cream with the garlic and thyme until warm. Remove from the heat and let cool.

Coat the inside of a shallow casserole dish no larger than 9 by 11 inches with nonstick spray. Place a layer of sliced potatoes on the bottom of the casserole dish. Lightly drizzle the potatoes with ⅓ cup cream and lightly sprinkle with cheese and a pinch of salt and pepper. Repeat this step three times.

After the third layer, cover the potatoes with one layer of apple, lightly drizzle the remaining cream, and sprinkle with cheese and a pinch of salt and pepper. Repeat this step using the yam, and then make one more layer of apple.

Finish the gratin with more layers of potato and then generously cover the top with the remaining cheese.

Cover the gratin with foil and bake for 1 hour. Remove the cover and bake for another hour or until you can easily slide a knife through the gratin. Place the prosciutto on top of the gratin and bake for an additional 10 minutes. Serve hot.

Red Chard, Cheddar, and Potato Gratin

Serves 12

The layers of this gratin are beautiful with the red Swiss chard. The last 15 minutes of baking give the gratin a nice crust of cheese.

3 pounds Yukon Gold potatoes, peeled and thoroughly dried
3 bunches (about 3 pounds) red Swiss chard, stems and leaves, well rinsed
¼ cup blended oil (page 7)
1 teaspoon chopped garlic
¼ cup white wine
salt and pepper
2 pounds white Cheddar, grated

nonstick cooking spray

Preheat the oven to 375°F.

Slice the potatoes to a 1/16-inch thickness with a mandoline.

Sauté the chard leaves in the oil with the garlic and white wine in a large sauté pan. Cook until the leaves are tender.

Blanch the chard stems in salted water until soft, about 5 minutes. Blanch the potatoes until just cooked but still firm, about 8 minutes. Allow all the ingredients to cool and be sure to drain as much liquid as possible from the potatoes and stems. Squeeze excess moisture from the chard leaves as well.

To make the gratin, coat the inside of a 9 x 11-inch baking pan with nonstick spray. Place the potatoes in one layer on the bottom of the pan. Season with salt and pepper and add a layer of cheese. Continue layering with chard leaves, cheese (use up about three-quarters of the cheese), potatoes, and chard stems, and season again with salt and pepper. Add another layer of potatoes and season once again.

Cover with foil and weight the pan down with a heavy pot. Bake for 1 hour. Remove from the oven, remove the weight, and add the remaining ½ pound of cheese. Bake uncovered for an additional 35 minutes. Let cool slightly before cutting.

Roasted Potatoes

SERVES 6

This is a basic and simple potato recipe that works with almost any large plate. The potatoes need almost no attention and the longer they cook, the crispier the skins. Be creative with the wide variety of potatoes in the markets today.

3 pounds potatoes (such as Yukon Gold and red)
2 tablespoons extra virgin olive oil
salt and pepper
2 teaspoons minced garlic
1 tablespoon chopped fresh thyme
1 tablespoon chopped fresh Italian parsley
1 teaspoon chopped fresh rosemary

Preheat the oven to 425°F.

Cut the potatoes in half lengthwise and then cut lengthwise again. Cut into 1-inch pieces, toss with the olive oil, and generously season with salt and pepper. Place the potatoes in a large roasting pan and roast for about 35 minutes. When the potatoes are just soft, toss with the garlic, thyme, parsley, and rosemary and roast for another 5 minutes. Adjust the seasoning.

Fingerling Potato Confit

SERVES 6

Confit as a cooking method means to cook something submerged in fat or oil. You may expect these potatoes to be overly oily, but they are not. They have a great texture, and garlic and thyme balance the potato taste.

2 pounds fingerling potatoes, cut in half and thoroughly dry
4 cups extra virgin olive oil
5 garlic cloves, peeled
3 thyme sprigs
1½ tablespoons salt
1 teaspoon pepper

Place the potatoes in a deep cooking pot. Add the olive oil, garlic, thyme, salt, and pepper. Make sure the potatoes are covered completely by the oil (add more oil if necessary). Heat the oil and cook the potatoes until soft, about 15 minutes. Remove from the heat and allow the potatoes to rest in the oil for at least 10 minutes. (The remaining oil can be saved and used several more times.)

Basil-Scented Potato Cakes

Makes 24 small bites or 12 large cakes

These cakes are so delicious they are impossible to resist. The fresh basil adds a fragrant essence to the potatoes and the creamy texture is due to the crème fraîche and the cheese. Try purple opal basil for a change in color.

- **4 russet potatoes, skin on**
- **1½ tablespoons crème fraîche (page 9)**
- **¼ pound Teleme cheese (cream cheese may be substituted)**
- **salt and white pepper**
- **½ bunch fresh basil, chopped (about 1 cup)**
- **2 eggs**
- **2 cups panko or dried bread crumbs**
- **1 cup blended oil (page 7)**

Preheat the oven to 375°F.

Place the potatoes on a baking sheet and bake until soft, about 1½ hours. When the potatoes are cool enough to handle, peel them and run them through a food mill or potato ricer. Add the crème fraîche and cheese and season with salt and pepper. Using your hands, work the basil into the potato mixture. Divide the potato mixture into 12 or 24 portions and form into cakes.

Place the eggs in a bowl and beat. Dip the cakes into the egg mixture and then into the panko.

Heat the oil to 325°F in a heavy-bottomed pan and pan-fry the potato cakes until golden brown, about 1½ minutes per side. Serve hot.

Mashed Potatoes

MAKES 3 CUPS

This recipe allows for half a cup of mashed potatoes per person. If I were you, I would double the recipe. These are so good that you'll want extra!

4 russet potatoes, peeled and cubed
⅔ cup heavy cream
4 tablespoons unsalted butter, at room temperature
1 tablespoon salt
¼ teaspoon white pepper

Place the potatoes in a pot, cover with cold water, and cook until soft, 15 to 20 minutes. Drain the potatoes and run them through a food mill or potato ricer.

Place the remaining ingredients in a saucepan and heat until the butter has melted into the cream.

Place the potatoes in a large bowl and, using a whisk, slowly work in the cream mixture. Once all the liquid has been added, whisk the potatoes until they have a nice light and fluffy texture. (Be careful not to overwhip or the potatoes will have a gluelike texture.) Adjust the seasoning.

Creamy Polenta

Serves 6

This is the perfect base for braised lamb or short ribs. We like to use a coarse polenta to add more of a crunch to the texture.

- 4 tablespoons (½ stick) unsalted butter
- 1 teaspoon minced garlic
- 3 cups heavy cream
- 1 tablespoon chopped fresh Italian parsley
- 1 tablespoon chopped fresh thyme
- 2 teaspoons chopped fresh sage
- salt and pepper
- 2 cups coarse polenta

In a large saucepan, heat the butter and sauté the garlic until golden brown. Add 5 cups water, the cream, and the herbs and season with salt and pepper. Bring the mixture to a boil. Whisk in the polenta and reduce the heat to a simmer. Cook, stirring frequently, until the polenta starts to pull away from the sides of the pan, 10 to 15 minutes. Adjust the seasoning and serve.

Risotto Cakes

Serves 6

We occasionally serve this as a side dish to accompany a hearty meat entree. Because risotto is time-consuming and requires constant attention, you may want to make this recipe with any type of leftover risotto. You can also serve these cakes as a main course with sauce and a salad, or serve smaller cakes at a cocktail party.

2 tablespoons olive oil
3 tablespoons minced shallots
2 cups Arborio rice
2 cups white wine
4 cups hot chicken stock (page 11)
salt
1 cup grated hard cheese
1 tablespoon fresh thyme
2 tablespoons chopped fresh Italian parsley
white pepper
2 cups panko (dried bread crumbs may be substituted)
½ cup blended oil (page 7)

Heat the olive oil in a sauté pan over medium heat and sauté the shallots until they are translucent. Stir in the rice and lightly toast it by stirring slowly and fairly constantly with a wooden spoon over moderately high heat until the grains begin to turn lightly golden.

Add the wine. Increase the heat and boil down the liquid. When the wine has almost evaporated and the rice is almost dry, ladle in enough hot stock to just cover the rice. Reduce the heat to a simmer, season with salt, and stir slowly and almost constantly for about 20 minutes. Continue to add the stock a little at a time as the rice absorbs it. After about 20 minutes, the risotto will be ready (the rice grains will have doubled in size and be suspended in a creamy liquid and the rice should be just tender).

Remove the rice from the heat and, with a wooden spoon, immediately stir in the cheese. Add the thyme and parsley. Season with white pepper to taste.

Spoon the risotto onto a baking sheet and cool in the refrigerator for about 20 minutes. After the risotto has cooled, form into flat cakes. Gently roll the cakes in panko and pan-fry in the oil until golden brown.

Food for thought *Serve with Wild Mushroom Ragout (page 182) or Roasted Tomato and Garlic Sauce (page 165).*

Citrus Pearl Couscous

Serves 6

If you can find pearl couscous, it is a great substitute for rice, pasta, or potatoes. It is quite simple to prepare and a fantastic base for a range of ingredients and flavors. This recipe is a terrific side dish for grilled or roasted fish.

2 tablespoons unsalted butter
½ onion, diced
juice and zest of 1 lemon
juice and zest of 2 oranges
2 tablespoons chopped fresh Italian parsley
1 tablespoon minced garlic
1½ cups pearl couscous, toasted
3 cups chicken stock (page 11)
1 tablespoon extra virgin olive oil
1 blood orange, segments only
1 orange, segments only
1 lime, segments only
salt and pepper

In a saucepan, melt the butter over medium heat and cook the onion until translucent. Add the citrus zest, parsley, and garlic and cook for several minutes. Add the couscous and mix well to coat with butter. Add the orange and lemon juice and simmer until reduced by half. Add the chicken stock and bring to a boil. Reduce the heat, cover, and let simmer until the liquid has evaporated, 12 to 14 minutes.

Transfer the couscous to a bowl and stir in the olive oil and citrus segments. Season with salt and pepper to taste. This dish can be served warm or cold.

Pearl Couscous and French Olives

Serves 6

For the past few years Sonoma has hosted the Olive Festival, a three-month span of olive-related events that include an olive oil tasting; a community olive pressing; a multicourse dinner prepared by local chefs featuring olives; a marketplace featuring olive products; and a martini contest. This salad is a tribute to the Olive Festival.

1 tablespoon salt
2 cups couscous (pearl or Israeli)
3 tablespoons extra virgin olive oil
⅓ cup olives, such as Niçoise or Lucque, pitted and chopped
⅓ cup chopped fresh Italian parsley
½ fennel bulb, chopped
1 carrot, peeled and chopped
½ medium red onion, chopped
2 tablespoons lemon zest (from 2 to 3 lemons)
¼ cup capers, drained, liquid reserved
2 teaspoons orange juice
2 teaspoons minced shallots
2 teaspoons chopped fresh tarragon
½ teaspoon Dijon mustard
½ teaspoon whole-grain mustard
1½ tablespoons honey
1 tablespoon Champagne vinegar
2 tablespoons blended oil (page 7)
salt and pepper
¼ cup pistachio nuts, toasted and chopped

Bring the salt and 3 cups water to a boil in a large saucepan and add the couscous. Reduce the heat to a simmer, cover, and cook until the liquid is absorbed, 8 to 10 minutes. Transfer the couscous to a bowl, mix well with the olive oil, and chill.

Mix the olives, parsley, fennel, carrot, onion, lemon zest, capers, 2 tablespoons of the caper liquid, the orange juice, shallots, tarragon, mustards, honey, vinegar, and oil in a large bowl. Add the couscous and mix well. Season with salt and pepper to taste. Toss with the pistachio nuts just before serving.

Food for Thought *Serve this as a side dish for fish or chicken or as a salad on top of field greens.*

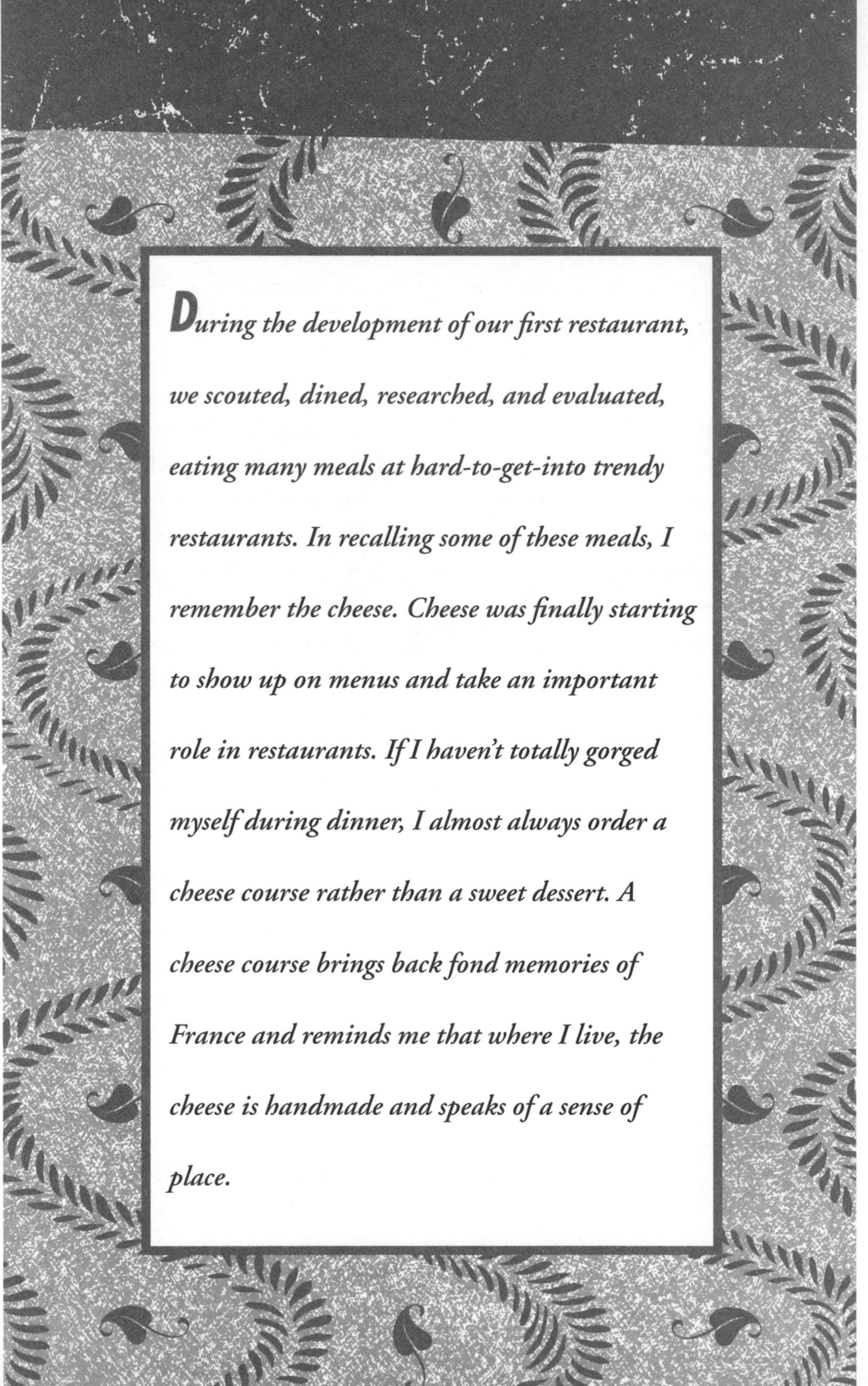

During the development of our first restaurant, we scouted, dined, researched, and evaluated, eating many meals at hard-to-get-into trendy restaurants. In recalling some of these meals, I remember the cheese. Cheese was finally starting to show up on menus and take an important role in restaurants. If I haven't totally gorged myself during dinner, I almost always order a cheese course rather than a sweet dessert. A cheese course brings back fond memories of France and reminds me that where I live, the cheese is handmade and speaks of a sense of place.

the girl & the fig cheese experience

Sonoma, California

Since we opened in 1997, we have offered our cheese courses at the beginning of the meal, with aged sausages and French olives or seasonal fruit and fig cake, or as a final course with a port pairing. The importance of sharing information about the cheese with the diner is critical. Each cheese course is served alongside a listing of the selected cheeses.

When the girl & the fig was located in Glen Ellen, the cheese was displayed on the table by the front door. As guests arrived, I enticed them with a visual presentation, and the cheese enticed them with heady aromas. For the first year, I lovingly put together almost every cheese plate that went out. Hefty slices and extra tastes went out to table after table. I also ate a bit of cheese myself. Being in charge of quality control is a hard job and someone has to do it! As business sense prevailed and we got smarter, we realized that the cheese course needed to be scaled back to smaller portions (not just for taste reasons but for cost reasons as well). I relinquished my duties and we bought a scale, ensuring the perfect amount of cheese on every plate.

We usually have at least twelve to fourteen cheeses in our kitchens at any given time. The cheeses we select vary from month to month. We categorize our selections by cow, goat, and sheep; by the United States and France; by soft, creamy, semifirm, and hard; and by light and milky to rich and intense. When serving a cheese course, offering a variety of tastes and textures is crucial, as well as serving the cheese at the proper temperature. We spend a good bit of time with our staff, training and tasting, so that they can assist our guests in choosing cheeses. Many guests review the list and make their own decisions, but others leave it up to the server.

On some nights, we also offer a cheese pairing. This dish varies from a very simple selection of cheese paired with roasted figs and balsamic reduction to more complicated plates, such as a savory blue cheese soufflé served with Syrah-poached cherries. The thoughtfulness of the accompaniments is an important part of our cheese plates.

The Artisan Cheese Makers

The cheese makers listed below all have a unique style and create award-winning cheeses, small artisan or farmstead cheeses that are not mass produced. Many of these cheeses are available directly from the dairy. Throughout the year, the flavors and textures of the cheeses change, because of aging, seasonality, and storage. There is a direct connection between what the cows, goats, and sheep eat and what kind of flavor the cheese imparts.

Bellwether Farms On the way to the Pacific Coast, in a very funky town called Valley Ford, is Bellwether Farms. The two-block town of Valley Ford can be described as rolling hills, rustic pastures, and ocean breezes. Creamy, rich, velvety, and grassy are all adjectives that come to mind when nibbling on Carmody, a cheese unique to Bellwether Farms. Carmody is generally aged at least six months, giving it layers of complexity, lingering flavors, and a silky texture.

Laura Chenel Chèvre, Inc. Laura Chenel is definitely a pioneer in goat cheese making in the United States. Having studied in France, she returned home with a deepened passion for the technique. Laura Chenel's cheeses vary from a very fresh chèvre in logs or tubs, Taupinière, chèvre marinated in olive oil, and six-month-aged goat's milk called Tome. Her Chef's Chèvre has been a mainstay in our kitchens since we opened. We use the Chef's Chèvre in our signature dish, the Grilled Fig Salad (page 98). We also use this cheese in omelets, pasta, and on our cheese platters. We are very lucky to have Laura Chenel right in our backyard!

Cowgirl Creamery Sue Conley of Cowgirl Creamery uses organic Straus Family Creamery milk to create artisan cheeses. The fromage blanc and crème fraîche are superb and we occasionally use them in our recipes. The Mt. Tam is a mold-ripened, triple crème disc. This cheese works especially well for our Goat Cheese Fritters (page 35). Mt. Tam has a flavor reminiscent of French brie but has a firm texture.

Cypress Grove This company was started by Mary Keehn, who decided to make cheese from her surplus of goat's milk. Her artisan cheeses are elegant, sophisticated, and original in flavor. The names of her cheeses exhibit her creativity even further.

Cheeses such as Humboldt Fog, Bermuda Triangle, and Mt. McKinley often find their way onto our cheese plates. One of her newer cheeses, called Midnight Moon, is a semifirm goat's milk, aged for at least one year. This cheese is mellow with a nutty flavor.

Joe Matos Cheese Company Joe and Mary Matos are the owners and cheese makers of Matos Cheese. They make a semihard, full-bodied cheese called St. George, a Portuguese-style cheese. This raw cow's milk farmhouse cheese has a flavor very similar to Cheddar.

Peluso Cheese, Inc. This company creates a semifirm and tangy cheese called Teleme, which is unique to California and came about as a feta-making mistake. This creamy cow's milk cheese is coated in an edible rice flour crust and is excellent to cook with.

Point Reyes Farmstead Cheese Company In 2000, the Giacomini family started producing California's first blue-veined cheese. Original Blue is made within hours of the early-morning milking and is then left to age for a minimum of six months. This technique creates a creamy, full-flavored blue cheese. It's made from cultured raw milk and is enhanced by the coastal fog and the salty Pacific breezes.

Redwood Hill Farm Jennifer Bice is the cheese maker and owner. Her goat's milk cheeses are very similar to the farmhouse cheeses of France. The Crottin, a small cheese with a likeness to the French cheese Crottin de Chavignol, is creamy, robust, and earthy with a natural edible golden-colored rind.

Three Sisters Farmstead Cheese Company This company creates an incredible hard cheese called Sareanah, with a taste between that of Parmesan and Gouda. Sareanah cheese is made from the morning milk of Jersey and Holstein cows. Aged for four to six months, these large twenty-pound wheels are rich and nutty with a dry texture.

Vella Cheese Company This company has been making cheese for over seventy years in Sonoma. The cows graze on the lush Sonoma grass in close proximity to the creamery. Our favorite cheese from Vella is the Special Reserve Dry Jack, which is aged for between eighteen and twenty-four months and exhibits deep, rich butterscotch flavors. This cheese is made with raw cow's milk and the wheels are uniquely coated with oil, cocoa, and black pepper. We serve the cheese on the cheese plate and cook with it as well.

Winchester Cheese Company Jules Wesselink, born in Holland, owns and operates this company. His California dairies, with more than five hundred Holsteins, date back to

the 1950s. Jules's daughter, Valerie, is the cheese maker. Winchester Gouda is made with all-natural ingredients and fresh raw milk. My favorite is the Medium-Aged Gouda, which is farm aged for a minimum of three months. It has a moderately sharp, nutty flavor with a grainy texture.

Yerba Santa Dairy When we are lucky we get a delivery of Alpine Shepherd's Cheese, the signature cheese made by this company in Lakeport. It is made with raw goat's milk and can be aged for up to fourteen months. This rustic cheese has a hard texture and the flavors are bold and robust.

For information on ordering these cheeses, see Sources, pages 251–52.

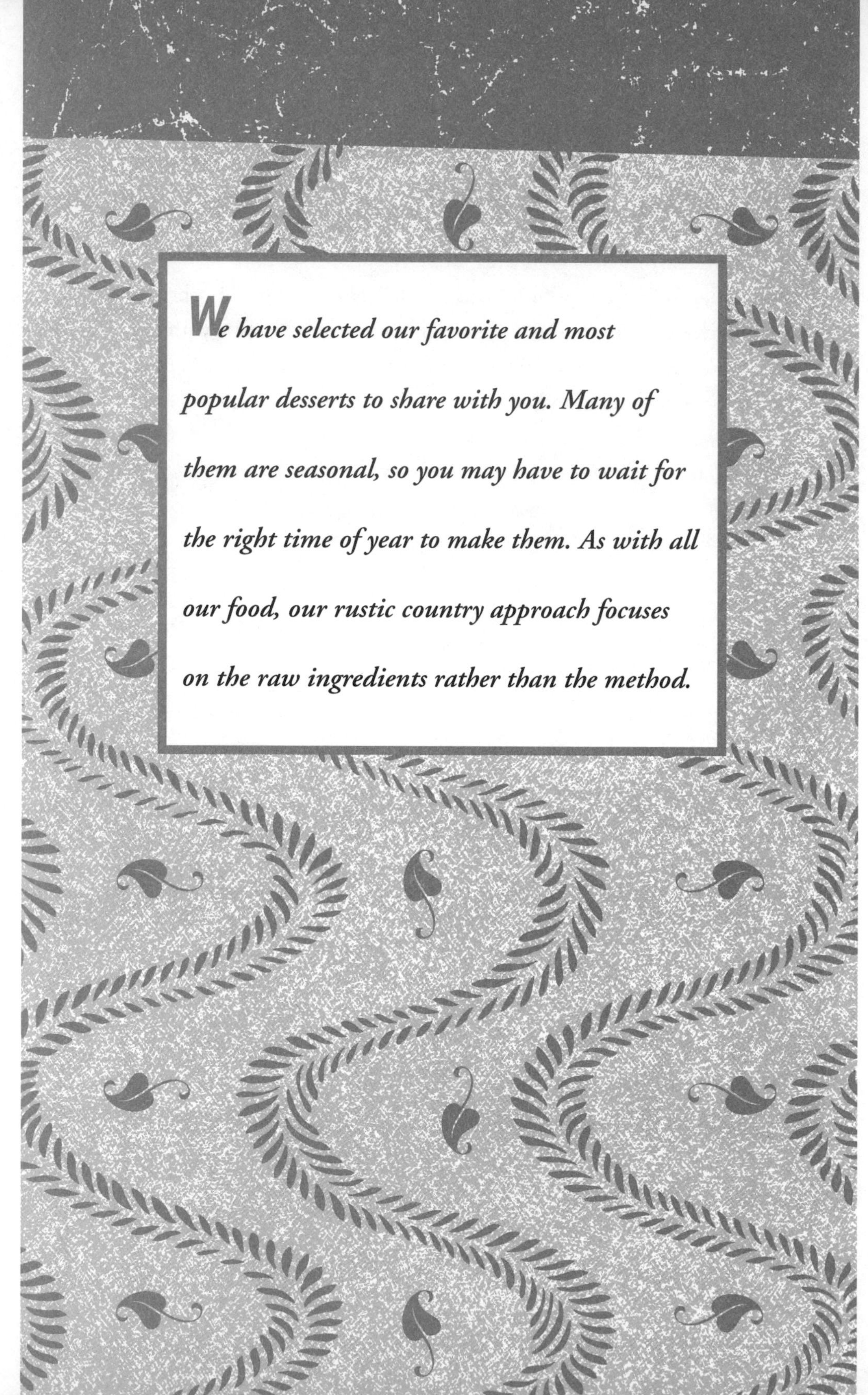

We have selected our favorite and most popular desserts to share with you. Many of them are seasonal, so you may have to wait for the right time of year to make them. As with all our food, our rustic country approach focuses on the raw ingredients rather than the method.

sweets

Sweet Goat Cheese–Stuffed Figs
Roasted Figs with Honey and Vanilla Ice Cream
Pear Clafouti
Brown Butter and Almond Cake with Berries
Cinnamon "Biscones" with Strawberries and Whipped Cream
Meyer Lemon Tartlets with Blood Orange Sauce
Warm Fig and Thyme Crisp with Fig Syrup
Mixed Nut Tart
Caramel Apple Tartlet with Vanilla Ice Cream
Chocolate Hazelnut Tart with Frangelico Cream
Profiteroles with Bittersweet Chocolate Sauce
Bellwether Farms Ricotta Cheesecake with Peaches and Cream
Pumpkin Cheesecake Tartlets
Lavender and Wildflower Honey Crème Brûlée
Savory Blue Cheese Soufflé with Syrah-Poached Cherries
Chocolate Pots de Crème
Lemon Shortbread Dough

Cupping the fig
In her small hand
The girl caresses
Its simple graceful form
Caresses it and studies it, absorbed
Marvels
At its dusky hue
Its yielding velvet softness
Promising such richness
She is almost afraid to taste

She too is a marvel
An equally miraculous creation
Though she has yet to discover it
Or is only beginning to forget
One who senses
The quality of ripeness
By a mechanism so subtle
It needs only a moment on her fingertips
One on whom
Already
The intensity of beauty
Has made an impact
Breaking her open again and again
One hose nature
Is to dive
Relentlessly
Into her own mysterious depths
Bearing to the surface
The drowning voice of her own awareness
She will blossom and become
A lover of the world
Who gives and yields
This gift
Her essence
Like a ripening fig

LENI ORTENBURGER, "ON THE OCCASION OF HER FIRST FIG"

Sweet Goat Cheese–Stuffed Figs

Serves 6

The doorbell rings and your neighbor appears on your doorstep with his favorite ten-year-old tawny port. You meander outside to your favorite fig tree and pluck some ripe figs. As you discuss work and the weather you whip up this simple recipe, and voilà!—figs and port.

12 large fresh figs
¾ cup goat cheese, at room temperature
2 tablespoons honey

Preheat the oven to 350°F.

Slice off the top third of the figs and set aside. Gently scoop out the fig flesh with a melon baller. Fill each fig with the goat cheese. Replace the fig tops and drizzle the figs with the honey. Roast for 12 minutes.

Wine pairing **Tawny Port**

Roasted Figs with Honey and Vanilla Ice Cream

Serves 6

You still have too many figs on your kitchen table and your best friend wants to take you to a last-minute dinner party. You were asked to bring dessert, but you are working until the last minute and have no time to spare. Visit a fig tree, grab a few figs, pick up a quart of vanilla ice cream on the way, and you will be the hit of the party!

12 fresh figs, halved
½ cup wildflower honey
cracked pepper

Preheat the oven to 350°F.

Drizzle the figs with ¼ cup of the honey and roast them for 10 minutes. Drizzle the remaining ¼ cup honey over the figs and crack fresh pepper over the top. Serve over vanilla ice cream.

Wine pairing **Late Harvest Viognier**

the fig farm

Sometimes in life, special things arrive and then disappear, leaving nothing but a vague memory. The Fig Farm was one of those things. In the beginning, I was fortunate enough to meet a wonderful couple who had a fig farm in the Napa Valley. Their farm was relatively small, about 225 trees. Mr. Fig, as I called him, would walk me through the fig orchard, or *les figuiers,* and proudly point out the different fig varietals. He had pruned them to about eight feet high so that he could reach the ripe figs without ladders and cranes.

I had a particular fondness for Mr. and Mrs. Fig, and we would take turns delivering and retrieving the figs. When I would go to pick them up, I felt as if I were an old family friend or perhaps their granddaughter. On one visit Mrs. Fig made a wonderful lunch of a salad with lovely fresh vegetables from her garden and a simple dish of polenta with sausage and tomato sauce. When they would deliver the figs, I made them come around noontime so that I could treat them to lunch. I loved to fuss over them.

Sometimes we would get two varietals of figs from them and sometimes we would get ten. They were lovingly lined up in rows with paper towels dividing each type of fig. Mr. Fig knew exactly which fig was which. I had to write down the different names as I tasted one of each.

This is how the fig flight began. During the one fig season that I knew Mr. and Mrs. Fig, we were able to serve a simple fig tasting, highlighting the flavors of the different figs. We served them with grilled prosciutto, a wedge of cheese, and some nuts.

Sadly enough, Mr. and Mrs. Fig couldn't maintain the farm, so they sold their property and the figs were removed and replaced with grapevines. I have lost touch with them and have not seen such beautiful figs since.

Pear Clafouti

Makes one 9-inch tart

A clafouti, a rustic French dessert, is a combination of a fruit tart and a pudding. This is a simple dessert to prepare, and it is not overly sweet. Serve it in the fall when pears are the ripest.

½ cup sugar
3 eggs
½ cup milk
½ cup heavy cream
1 cup flour
½ teaspoon salt
1 teaspoon vanilla extract
1 tablespoon framboise
1 large pear, thinly sliced

nonstick cooking spray

Preheat the oven to 350°F.

Whisk the sugar and eggs together in a bowl. Heat the milk and cream in a saucepan and bring to a boil. Slowly whisk the cream mixture into the egg mixture. Slowly whisk in the flour until incorporated. Add the salt, vanilla, and framboise.

Spray a 9 by 11-inch baking pan with nonstick spray or use a nonstick pan. Place half the pear slices on the bottom of the pan and pour the batter over them. Put the remaining pears on top. Bake for 50 to 60 minutes or until a knife comes out clean from the center.

Wine pairing **Late Harvest Viognier**

Food for thought *This dessert is also fantastic with fresh figs (8 large figs, sliced in half), cherries (½ pound, pitted), or Santa Rosa plums (3 plums, pitted and thinly sliced).*

Brown Butter and Almond Cake with Berries

Makes one 10-inch cake

This is a rich and flavorful cake due entirely to the brown butter. It is an excellent cake for fresh fruit. We serve it with berries, but warm peaches, caramelized bananas, or sautéed apples would work as well.

¾ pound (3 sticks) unsalted butter
2 vanilla beans
1 pound confectioners' sugar
¾ cup blanched almonds, finely ground
¾ cup flour
15 egg whites
6 cups mixed berries (about 3 pints), cleaned, large berries quartered
½ cup framboise (cassis may be substituted)
1 cup granulated sugar

nonstick cooking spray

Preheat the oven to 375°F.

Place the butter in a saucepan and cook over low heat until dark brown. Remove from the heat and strain. Keep warm.

Scrape the seeds from the vanilla beans and mix with the confectioners' sugar, almonds, flour, and warm butter in a large bowl. Mix thoroughly.

In a separate bowl, whip the egg whites until stiff but not dry. Gently fold the whites in batches into the flour mixture.

Line the bottom of a 10-inch springform pan with parchment paper and coat with nonstick spray. Pour in the batter. Bake for 1 hour or until a knife comes out clean. Let cool.

Place the berries, framboise, and granulated sugar in a small saucepan and cook for 5 minutes over low heat. Remove from the heat and serve over the cake.

Wine pairing **Late Harvest Viognier**

Food for thought *This cake can also be made in a rectangular baking pan. Once it's baked, you can cut squares, triangles, or other shapes with a cookie cutter.*

Cinnamon "Biscones" with Strawberries and Whipped Cream

Serves 6

This is our version of strawberry shortcake. The main ingredient is our special creation, which we call a "biscone," a cross between a biscuit and a scone.

Biscones

- 2 cups flour
- ¼ cup granulated sugar
- 4 teaspoons baking powder
- zest of 1 orange, grated
- pinch of cinnamon
- 2 egg yolks, hard-boiled and mashed with a fork
- 6 tablespoons unsalted butter, chilled and cut into 1-inch cubes
- ¾ cup heavy cream
- ¼ cup rolled oats

Topping

- ¼ cup rolled oats, toasted
- 1 tablespoon light brown sugar
- ⅛ teaspoon cinnamon

Strawberries

- 4 cups strawberries (2 pints)
- 1-inch long cinnamon stick
- ¾ cup simple syrup (page 8)
- 2 teaspoons Cointreau (Triple Sec may be substituted)
- 2 tablespoons lime juice

Whipped cream

- ½ cup heavy cream
- ½ cup crème fraîche (page 9)
- ½ teaspoon almond extract
- ⅓ cup confectioners' sugar

Preheat the oven to 350°F.

To make the biscones, in a food processor mix the flour, sugar, and baking powder. Add the orange zest, cinnamon, and egg yolks. Pulse three times. Add the butter and pulse until it breaks up in the mixture. Add 6 tablespoons of the cream in three additions, pulsing between each addition. Turn the dough out onto a floured surface, pour the oats evenly over the dough, and knead until the dough just comes together. Do not overwork it. Roll out the dough to 1-inch thickness and cut out rounds using a 3-inch cookie cutter. Place the dough rounds on a parchment-lined baking sheet.

To prepare the biscone topping, place the toasted oats in a food processor with the brown sugar and cinnamon. Process until the oats are one-quarter of their original size. Brush the dough rounds with the remaining 2 tablespoons cream and sprinkle with the oat and sugar mixture. Bake for 50 minutes. Remove from the oven and set aside.

Slice 1 cup of the strawberries and place in a saucepan with the cinnamon stick, simple syrup, 1 teaspoon of the Cointreau, and the lime juice. Simmer for 10 minutes over medium heat, then remove and strain the mixture through a chinoise or fine mesh sieve into another saucepan. Discard the solids. Reduce the liquid by one-quarter. Chill and set aside.

In a separate bowl, slice the remaining 3 cups strawberries and add the remaining 1 teaspoon Cointreau.

Place the cream, crème fraîche, almond extract, and confectioners' sugar in a bowl and whip until stiff.

Cut the biscones in half horizontally. On the bottom half, layer strawberries and whipped cream. Cover with the top half and spoon more strawberries on top with a dollop of whipped cream. Drizzle with the reduced strawberry sauce.

WINE PAIRING Muscat or Grand Marnier

Meyer Lemon Tartlets with Blood Orange Sauce

SERVES 6

Sometimes you want something sweet after dinner that won't quite take you over the edge. For me this would be almost any lemon dessert. Simple and quick to prepare, these tartlets are a winner every time, and the Meyer lemons set them apart from regular lemon tarts.

½ recipe Lemon Shortbread Dough (page 235)

Meyer lemon curd

2 cups confectioners' sugar
1¼ cups Meyer lemon juice (from about 5 lemons)
6 eggs
10 tablespoons unsalted butter, melted
pinch of turmeric

Blood Orange Sauce

1½ cups blood orange juice (from 7 to 8 oranges)
2 cups orange juice
¼ cup grenadine
½ star anise

Candied Citrus (recipe follows)

Preheat the oven to 325°F.

To make the lemon curd, in a large bowl mix the sugar and lemon juice until the sugar is dissolved. Lightly beat the eggs and add to the lemon mixture. Add the melted butter and turmeric and mix well. Cook the mixture in a stainless steel pot over low heat, stirring constantly with a wooden spoon until the lemon mixture begins to thicken. Do not bring to a boil! Strain the lemon mixture through a chinoise or fine mesh sieve. Place the pot in an ice-water bath and stir the mixture until it has cooled.

Fill six 3½-inch tart shells and bake for 10 to 12 minutes or until set.

To make the sauce, combine the blood orange juice, orange juice, grenadine, and star anise in a small saucepan. Reduce to 1 cup over medium heat. Strain and cool. Place the tartlet on a plate and drizzle with the sauce. Garnish with Candied Citrus.

Candied Citrus

1 orange peel, cut in 1/8-inch strips
1 lemon peel, cut in 1/8-inch strips
1 cup simple syrup (page 8)
1/4 cup sugar

Preheat oven to 200° F.

Place orange and lemon peel strips in a large saucepan and cover with simple syrup. Bring to a low simmer and cook for 15 minutes. Drain and toss with sugar. Leave out overnight uncovered.

WINE PAIRING **Late Harvest Viognier**

FOOD FOR THOUGHT *Eliminate the crust and serve the lemon curd in a bowl with fresh blackberries and whipped cream.*

Warm Fig and Thyme Crisp with Fig Syrup

MAKES ONE 9 BY 12-INCH CRISP

This is one of our signature desserts. Because fig season is so limited, we make the jam for the filling with dried Adriatic figs. In season, we use fresh figs. We serve our crisp with Fig Syrup and Fig and Port ice cream, which is made exclusively for us by Ciao Bella.

Pastry

- 2 cups walnut halves
- 6 tablespoons plus ¾ cup granulated sugar
- ¾ cup packed light brown sugar
- 1½ teaspoons salt
- 1½ teaspoons baking powder
- 4½ cups flour
- ¾ pound (3 sticks) unsalted butter, thinly sliced
- 3 teaspoons vanilla extract
- 3 egg yolks

Jam

- 2½ pounds dried figs
- ¾ cup granulated sugar
- zest of 3 lemons, grated
- 1 bunch thyme, tied with twine
- 3 tablespoons lemon juice

Fig Syrup (recipe follows)

Preheat the oven to 350°F.

In a food processor, grind the walnuts (until medium-fine) with the 6 tablespoons granulated sugar and set aside. In an electric mixer, mix the ¾ cup granulated sugar, the brown sugar, salt, baking powder, and flour until well combined. Add the butter and mix until the mixture clumps, about 1½–2 minutes. Add the vanilla and egg yolks to the mixture and mix for 40 seconds. Pack two-thirds of the dough into the bottom of a 9 by 12-inch ungreased pan and bake until the dough is light brown, 25 to 30 minutes.

To make the jam, in a heavy-bottomed pot, combine the figs, sugar, lemon zest, thyme, and lemon juice and pour in enough water to cover. Bring to a boil and boil for 10 minutes. Reduce the heat and simmer until the figs are tender, about 30 minutes. Remove the thyme. Puree the mixture in a food processor until smooth.

To assemble the crisp, spread the jam evenly over the baked dough. In a bowl, crumble together the remaining third of the dough and the walnut and sugar mixture. Sprinkle the mixture over the fig jam and bake for 50 minutes. Drizzle with Fig Syrup (recipe follows).

Fig Syrup

MAKES ¾ CUP

5 dried Black Mission figs, stems removed, figs sliced
4 cups (750 ml bottle) ruby port
1 cinnamon stick
1 clove
½ cup sugar

Heat the figs, port, cinnamon stick, and clove in a saucepan over medium heat and reduce to ½ cup. Strain the sauce, pressing on the figs to get as much juice as possible. Whisk in the sugar and cool.

WINE PAIRING **Tawny Port**
FOOD FOR THOUGHT ***You can make individual crisps in small baking dishes using the same method.***

Mixed Nut Tart

MAKES ONE 11-INCH TART

We couldn't decide which nut to use for this tart, so we used a combination of nuts. This tart is best right out of the oven, but it tastes great reheated the next day. The nuts called for are whole, but you can chop them up if you prefer.

½ cup light brown sugar
½ cup granulated sugar
1 cup light corn syrup
1 teaspoon vanilla extract
3 tablespoons brown butter (page 8)
2 eggs
2 egg yolks
¾ cup pistachios, toasted
¾ cup pecans, toasted
½ cup walnuts, toasted
¼ cup hazelnuts, toasted and skinned
½ recipe Lemon Shortbread Dough (page 235)

Preheat the oven to 350°F.

In an electric mixer using a paddle attachment, combine the sugars, corn syrup, and vanilla and mix on low speed until the sugar is dissolved, 5 to 8 minutes. Add the brown butter and then add the eggs. Mix well and add the nuts. Spread the mixture in a thin layer in an 11-inch tart shell. (The filling should fill the tart shell three-quarters full.) Let sit for 10 minutes. Bake until firm and not liquid in the center, about 35 minutes. Serve warm with vanilla or caramel ice cream.

WINE PAIRING **Tawny Port**

FOOD FOR THOUGHT *To change the flavor of this tart, you can add toasted coconut or a layer of chocolate, or drizzle caramel sauce (see page 220) over the top.*

Caramel Apple Tartlet with Vanilla Ice Cream

MAKES 6 TARTLETS

This dessert is a cross between a caramel apple and a tarte Tatin.

6 Fuji apples, peeled
1¾ cups brandy
1¼ cups plus ⅔ cup sugar
1 sheet puff pastry
1 egg, beaten
½ cup heavy cream
2 tablespoons unsalted butter

Preheat the oven to 400°F.

Cut the tops and bottoms off the apples so they are flat on each end. Remove the apple cores without breaking the apples. Combine the brandy, the 1¼ cups sugar, and 1¼ cups water in a saucepan and bring to a boil. Place the apples in the boiling mixture and boil for 3 minutes. Remove the apples from the saucepan and cool. Reduce the poaching liquid to 1 cup.

Cut six 4-inch circles out of the puff pastry sheet. Place the pastry circles on a parchment-lined baking sheet or Silpat mat. Place an apple in the middle of each puff pastry circle. Brush the apples with the reduced poaching liquid and bake for 15 minutes. Remove from the oven and gently brush each apple and pastry with the beaten egg. Bake for an additional 20 minutes or until golden brown.

Meanwhile, to make the caramel sauce, heat the ⅔ cup sugar in a nonreactive pan over medium heat until well caramelized. Remove from the heat and add the cream. Stir until well incorporated. Add the butter and stir until smooth. Strain and set aside.

Remove the tartlets from the oven and fill the center of each apple with caramel sauce. Serve the tartlets with vanilla ice cream.

WINE PAIRING **Tawny Port**

Chocolate Hazelnut Tart with Frangelico Cream

MAKES ONE 11-INCH TART

This dessert should be called a "chocolate truffle tart." Need I say more?

Dough

- 1 cup flour
- ½ cup hazelnuts, toasted, skinned, and finely ground
- ⅓ cup unsweetened cocoa powder
- ¼ cup granulated sugar
- pinch of salt
- ¼ pound (1 stick) unsalted butter, chilled and cut into 1-inch cubes
- ¼ cup milk
- 1 teaspoon vanilla extract

Filling

- 2 cups heavy cream
- ⅓ cup cold espresso
- ⅓ cup granulated sugar
- ¼ teaspoon salt
- 8 ounces semisweet or bittersweet chocolate, chopped
- 2 teaspoons Frangelico (1 teaspoon hazelnut extract may be substituted)
- 1 egg
- 2 egg yolks

Whipped cream

- ½ cup heavy cream
- ½ tablespoon Frangelico (½ teaspoon hazelnut extract may be substituted)
- 1½ tablespoons confectioners' sugar

Preheat the oven to 400°F.

To make the dough, put the flour, hazelnuts, cocoa powder, granulated sugar, and salt in a food processor and pulse until well combined. Add the butter and pulse until the butter has broken up. Add the milk and vanilla and pulse until the dough just comes together. (If the dough is too dry add a bit of milk.)

Chill the dough for 1 hour and then roll it out to line an 11-inch tart shell. Chill for 15 minutes and prick with a fork. Blind bake (cover tart with parchment paper and dried beans) for 10 minutes. Remove the parchment and beans and bake for another 5 minutes or until firm in the center.

To make the filling, reduce the oven temperature to 350°F. In a saucepan, combine the cream, coffee, granulated sugar, and salt. Bring to a boil and then remove from the heat.

Add the chocolate and Frangelico and allow the chocolate to melt. Stir to combine. Whisk the eggs well and add to the chocolate mixture.

Strain the mixture through a chinoise, or other sieve with a very fine mesh, and pour into the tart shell. Bake for 20 minutes or until the filling starts to set. (Do not overbake this dessert; it may look as if it is not set, but it will set while chilling.) Chill in the refrigerator for at least 3 hours.

Whip together the cream, Frangelico, and confectioners' sugar until stiff. Cut the tart into 6 wedges and place on plates. Top each wedge with a dollop of the Frangelico Cream.

WINE PAIRING Syrah

FOOD FOR THOUGHT *Serve with Syrah-Poached Cherries (page 232) or berries.*

Profiteroles with Bittersweet Chocolate Sauce

Serves 6

Profiteroles are basically cream puffs, but what delicious cream puffs they are. We make these every day in the restaurant. I look for them on the rolling rack after they have been baked and can never resist sneaking just one. The kitchen staff is usually short one for their orders, but I never confess.

We slice the cream puffs in half and fill them with Ciao Bella's Tahitian Vanilla ice cream, then drizzle Bittersweet Chocolate Sauce over the top. The profiteroles can be made ahead and frozen. Reheat in a 325°F oven for 10 minutes before you are ready to serve them. This chocolate sauce will also keep refrigerated for several weeks, great for that late-night ice cream craving.

1 teaspoon salt
4 tablespoons (½ stick) unsalted butter
1 cup flour
5 eggs
Bittersweet Chocolate Sauce (recipe follows)

Preheat the oven to 350°F.

Combine 1 cup water with the salt and butter in a saucepan and bring to a boil. Turn the heat to medium-low, melt the butter, and stir in the flour all at once. Stir until well incorporated. Over very low heat, dry out the mixture slightly for 3 to 4 minutes, stirring constantly. Take the mixture off the heat and let cool for 10 to 15 minutes.

Place the flour mixture in an electric mixer and while mixing, add 4 of the eggs, one at a time, allowing time between each addition for the egg to incorporate into the dough.

Place the mixture in a pastry bag and chill in the refrigerator for 30 minutes. Divide the dough into 12 portions on a parchment-lined baking sheet. Lightly beat the remaining egg and brush a little on each profiterole. Bake for 50 minutes. Slice the profiteroles in half, place a scoop of vanilla ice cream on the bottom half, and replace the top half. Drizzle with Bittersweet Chocolate Sauce.

Bittersweet Chocolate Sauce

Makes 1¼ cups

- **½ cup heavy cream**
- **¼ cup corn syrup**
- **½ tablespoon vanilla extract**
- **½ pound bittersweet chocolate, chopped**

Heat the cream, corn syrup, vanilla, and 2 tablespoons water in a saucepan and bring to a boil. Place the chopped chocolate in a bowl and add the hot cream mixture. Stir until the chocolate is melted and the cream mixture is incorporated. To thin the chocolate sauce, add warm water 1 tablespoon at a time until the desired consistency is reached.

Wine pairing **Framboise**

Bellwether Farms Ricotta Cheesecake with Peaches and Cream

MAKES ONE 9-INCH CAKE

When looking for a not-so-sweet dessert for a wine dinner, we usually choose this recipe. Sometimes it is best to let the wine shine and allow the dessert to round out the flavors.

Cheesecake

8 eggs
¼ cup granulated sugar
3 pounds Bellwether Farms Ricotta, drained (either cow's or sheep's milk; see Sources, page 251)
3 tablespoons flour
2 teaspoons salt
6 tablespoons honey
zest of 2 lemons, grated
⅓ recipe Lemon Shortbread Dough (page 235), baked in the bottom of a 9-inch springform pan

Peaches

1 cup simple syrup (page 8)
½ cup lime juice
1 cinnamon stick
½ vanilla bean
4 peaches, cut into 1-inch slices
1 tablespoon framboise

Whipped cream

½ cup heavy cream
½ cup crème fraîche (page 9)
⅓ cup confectioners' sugar

Preheat the oven to 400°F.

To make the cheesecake, beat the eggs and granulated sugar together in an electric mixer until the mixture is light and pale. Add the ricotta, flour, salt, honey, and lemon zest and mix until light and fluffy. Fill the baked crust in the springform pan with the ricotta mixture and bake for 50 minutes.

Combine the syrup, lime juice, cinnamon stick, and vanilla bean in a nonreactive pan and bring to a boil over medium heat. Reduce the liquid by a third.

Place the peaches in a bowl and toss them with the framboise and the hot syrup. Place them in the refrigerator and let cool. Remove the cinnamon stick and vanilla bean. Bring to room temperature before serving.

Place the cream, crème fraîche, and confectioners' sugar in a bowl and whip until stiff. Slice the cheesecake and serve with the peaches and whipped cream.

WINE PAIRING **Late Harvest Viognier or Muscat**

FOOD FOR THOUGHT *You can also serve this cheesecake with Syrah-Poached Cherries (page 232).*

Arise, my love, my fair one, and come away; for now the winter is past, the rain is over and gone. The flowers appear on the earth; the time of singing has come, and the voice of the turtledove is heard in our land. The fig tree puts forth its figs, and the vines are in blossom; they give forth fragrance. Arise, my love, my fair one, and come away.

SONG OF SOLOMON 2:10–13.

Pumpkin Cheesecake Tartlets

Serves 6

What is autumn without some kind of pumpkin dessert? Cloves, nutmeg, ginger, and cinnamon are the usual suspects when seasoning pumpkin puree and here they make a delicious fall cheesecake. It can be made as a whole cheesecake or as the tartlets we describe below.

1 pound cream cheese
¾ cup granulated sugar
1 cup heavy cream
¾ cup crème fraîche (page 9)
1 egg
2 egg yolks
1 vanilla bean, scraped
2 tablespoons lemon juice
1½ cups canned pumpkin puree
⅓ cup light brown sugar, packed
½ teaspoon ground cloves
½ teaspoon white pepper
1 teaspoon ground nutmeg
1 teaspoon ground ginger
2 teaspoons ground cinnamon
½ recipe Lemon Shortbread Dough (page 235)
confectioners' sugar
whipped cream

Preheat the oven to 300°F.

In a food processor mix the cream cheese and granulated sugar until smooth. Add the cream, crème fraîche, egg, egg yolks, vanilla, and lemon juice. Add the pumpkin puree, brown sugar, and spices. Ladle the pumpkin mixture into six 4-inch tartlet shells. Bake for about 30 minutes or until set. Sprinkle each tartlet with confectioners' sugar and serve with whipped cream.

Wine pairing **Mulled wine**

Lavender and Wildflower Honey Crème Brûlée

Makes 6 servings

Simple custard is a perfect way to experiment with flavor. In the restaurant we have served several versions of this dessert, including chocolate-orange and vanilla bean, but our lavender crème brûlée brings our guests back. As you crack through the thin layer of sugar and take your first taste, you will be delighted by the unexpectedly perfumed flavor and velvety texture of this custard.

- **2¼ cups heavy cream**
- **¾ cup milk**
- **3 or 4 lavender sprigs or 1½ tablespoons dried lavender plus lavender blossoms for garnish**
- **8 egg yolks**
- **½ cup sugar plus about 4 tablespoons sugar for sprinkling**
- **2 tablespoons wildflower honey**

Preheat the oven to 350°F.

Place the cream and milk in a saucepan and add the lavender. Bring to a boil and turn off the heat. Let the lavender stems steep for about 15 minutes or until the milk has a lavender flavor. (For a stronger flavor, allow to steep longer.) Meanwhile, beat the egg yolks, the ½ cup sugar, and the honey until smooth. Whisk into the lavender-cream mixture. Strain through a fine-mesh sieve and skim off any foam. Refrigerate for at least 4 hours.

Pour the mixture into 6 ramekins or crème brûlée dishes. Set the ramekins in a baking pan and add enough hot water to reach halfway up the sides of the ramekins. Cover the baking pan with foil and place in the oven. Bake for 40 minutes or until set. (Test for doneness by jiggling the ramekins.) Remove the baking pan from the oven and allow the ramekins to cool in the water bath for 5 minutes. Refrigerate for a few hours or overnight.

Before serving, sprinkle the tops with a thin layer of sugar and caramelize with a small torch or under a broiler set on high. Garnish each crème brûlée with lavender blossoms.

Wine pairing **Late Harvest Viognier**

Savory Blue Cheese Soufflé with Syrah-Poached Cherries

Serves 6

We occasionally serve this as a cheese pairing when we want to highlight a special blue cheese. When you first taste this soufflé, you will be surprised at the outcome—delicious, but not what you may have expected.

Soufflé

3 tablespoons unsalted butter
3 tablespoons flour
1 cup milk
3 egg yolks
½ cup blue cheese (preferably Point Reyes Original Blue)
4 egg whites

nonstick cooking spray

Cherries

2 cups Syrah (any dry, full-bodied red wine may be substituted)
2 cups simple syrup (page 8)
1 cup dried cherries
1 vanilla bean
1 cinnamon stick

Preheat the oven to 350°F.

Over medium heat, melt the butter in a large saucepan. Add the flour and stir constantly until the mixture is smooth. Add the milk and bring to a boil; stir until smooth. Let stand for 1 minute to cool. In a stainless steel bowl, lightly beat the egg yolks and add the cheese. Slowly add the milk mixture and set aside.

In another stainless steel bowl, whisk the egg whites until stiff but not dry. Fold the egg whites with a spatula into the cheese and milk mixture. Spray six 3½-inch soufflé ramekins with nonstick spray; fill the ramekins three-quarters full. Bake for 30 minutes or until lightly golden. The soufflés should rise about 1½ inches over the tops of the ramekins. Let cool. At once transfer the soufflés from the ramekins to a plate. Serve immediately.

To prepare the cherries, in a saucepan simmer the Syrah, syrup, dried cherries, vanilla bean, and cinnamon stick for 10 minutes. Remove the cherries and reduce the liquid to

1 cup. Remove the vanilla bean and cinnamon stick and return the cherries to the sauce. Spoon the sauce over the cheese soufflés.

WINE PAIRING **Syrah**

FOOD FOR THOUGHT *This soufflé can also be served with a savory sauce as an appetizer. Try the Tomato Cream Sauce (page 167) or the Dried Cherry and Peppercorn Sauce (page 166).*

Chocolate Pots de Crème

SERVES 6

Several years ago, when dining in a friend's restaurant, I ordered the chocolate pot de crème. Though I was sharing this dessert with my dining companions, I became very possessive and actually ordered a second one just for myself. This chocolate custard was so divine that I wanted our restaurant guests to experience it. So later that week, we cooked up our own version of this delectable, sinful pot of chocolate. Served with an espresso whipped cream, this is a perfect ending to any meal!

1 cup milk
¾ cup heavy cream
7 ounces bittersweet chocolate, roughly chopped
1 teaspoon vanilla extract
6 egg yolks
⅓ cup sugar

Preheat the oven to 350°F.

Place the milk and cream in a saucepan and bring to a boil. Remove from the heat. Add the chocolate and vanilla, cover, and allow the chocolate to melt. In a large bowl, whisk the egg yolks and sugar. Remove any foam. Stir the chocolate mixture until smooth and consistent and slowly whisk it into the egg mixture. Strain the mixture and chill until cool, about 1 hour.

Place 6 ramekins in a baking pan. Fill the ramekins with the chocolate mixture and pour boiling water into the baking pan. Cover the pan with foil. Bake in the water bath for about 1 hour or until just set. Eat straight from the oven, or refrigerate for 2 hours and then serve.

WINE PAIRING Framboise

Lemon Shortbread Dough

MAKES
THREE 9-INCH RICOTTA CHEESECAKES *(page 226)*
TWO 11-INCH MIXED NUT TARTS *(page 219)*
TWELVE 3-INCH MEYER LEMON TARTLETS *(page 214)*

This is extraordinary, versatile dough. Simple to make, it is our standard dough for most of our tarts and cheesecakes. We recommend that you make a batch or two of this dough, portion it out in various sizes, and keep it in the freezer for future baking.

14 tablespoons (7 ounces) unsalted butter
½ cup sugar
1 egg
1 egg yolk
¼ teaspoon salt
zest of 1 lemon, grated
1 teaspoon vanilla extract
2½ cups flour

In a food processor, cream the butter and sugar. Add the egg, egg yolk, salt, lemon zest, and vanilla. Add the flour to the butter and egg mixture. Form the dough into a ball and refrigerate for at least 12 hours.

Preheat the oven to 350°F.

Roll the dough out to the desired shape (depends on pan size). Prick the dough with a fork and bake for 12 to 15 minutes.

a word about wine

When in Rhône, well, not exactly Rhône

Over the last twenty years California has become one of the finest wine-producing regions in the world. Its reputation has been built largely on the Chardonnay and Cabernet Sauvignon grown primarily in Napa and Sonoma counties. The amazing transformation in the California wine industry is a tribute to the foresight and efforts of individuals who believed that California wine would be equal to any wine produced elsewhere in the world. Now, as we progress through the new millennium, an increasing number of grape varieties are gaining respect from the average American wine drinker. Local winemakers are currently turning their attention back to long-forgotten varieties. These wines are being made with the same innovation and style that California winemakers used to shock the wine world in the 1970s with Chardonnay and Cabernet. The girl & the fig toasts these winemakers in their untiring efforts to make the best wine possible in their own incomparable California style.

Many confused looks have been produced by our wine list. Instead of the usual Cabernet and Chardonnay wines, it is a list of Rhône-styled California wines. We put a lot of thought into our wine list. It would have been far easier to simply collect a group of excellent Chardonnay, Zinfandel, and Pinot Noir wines, but we wanted a sophisticated list with a theme that would pair nicely with our menu.

With this in mind, it was off to the Rhône we went—the California Rhône, that is. We chose the varietals of the Rhône for many reasons, but foremost was their compatibility with our food. We needed wines that would not be overshadowed by our food but would enhance and define our creations. The explosive and seductive scent of a Viognier paired with mussels is something that everyone should experience. We also saw the ability to create a truly unique dining experience in which a guest could discover a little bit about wine while at the restaurant, and that is how our "flight program" came to be. Both for fun and

in all seriousness, we offer our guests the opportunity to taste three different wines of the same varietals, such as Syrah or Viognier, or three to five different varietals, such as Roussanne, Marsanne, Mourvèdre, Cinsault, or Carignane. With a list in hand, guests can compare the nuances of the wines and taste how each reacts with the food. Many of our guests have enjoyed this approach and fallen in love with wines they had previously never heard of. It is incredibly satisfying to know that our friends and guests enjoy their meals, but it is even better knowing that they might learn or discover something new during their dinner. The profiles of the Rhône grape varietals listed below are an incorporation of tasting notes and our opinions.

Carignane

Carignane (the California spelling) grapes make red wines typically rich in flavor because of their concentrated fruit. They are deep in color and high in tannins and alcohol. These wines are big, bold, and robust. My favorite wines made from the Carignane grape come from Spain, in the Priorat region, where Carignan is carefully blended with Grenache, or Garnacha (as it is called in Spain), to produce lovely, lyrical, multidimensional wines that hog the spotlight during a meal.

Nose chocolate, clove, cedar, nutmeg
Mouthfeel high tannins, high alcohol
Flavors fruity, spicy, dusty berries, earthy fruit
Featured California producers Fife Vineyards, Cline Cellars, Ravenswood
Food pairings Pan-Seared Beef Fillet with Tarragon Butter, Liberty Duck Breast with Sonoma Mustard Sauce, Pan-Seared Lamb Medallions with Roasted Garlic Aïoli

Cinsault

Of all the Rhône varietals, Cinsault is the least known and most ellusive. Like Marsanne, not many wines are made using this grape, and often Cinsault is blended with other wines to add another flavor dimension. The true Cinsaults are a pleasure. Castle Vineyards and Frick consistently produce fine examples year after year. Cinsaults complement a meal of many elements. This is a red wine that can be easily consumed without fear of a big wine headache the next day!

Nose berries, lavender, anise
Mouthfeel light in body, high acidity, low tannins
Flavors spicy cherry, strawberries, spice, earth
Featured California producers Castle Vineyards, Frick Winery
Food pairings Polenta Cakes, Goat Cheese Fritters, Rabbit and Hazelnut Pâté, White Bean and Duck Confit Soup, Wild Mushroom Risotto, Coq au Vin, Duck Confit, Pan-Seared Calf's Liver

Grenache

I am particularly fond of wines made with the Grenache grape because they pair perfectly with my favorite foods. This is a wine that understands sharing and doesn't need to take center stage as so many other wines do.

The Grenache grape is used in many white and red wines throughout the world. In Provence, the famous rosé wines brighten any lunch. Along the Rhône, the Gigondas wines are explosive and sensuous but soften as they age. In Spain, where Grenache is known as Garnacha, it is blended with Carignan, resulting in some of the best and most unique wines available today.

Nose spicy, minerally
Mouthfeel amazing density, racy acidity
Flavors lush and rich, berry fruit, ripe blackberry fruit, herbal notes
Featured California producers Jaffurs Wine Cellars, Philip Staley Vineyards & Winery
Food pairings Chicken Liver Mousse, Pork and Dried Cherry Pâté, Pan-Roasted Monkfish with Clams, Grilled Salmon with Lavender Beurre Rouge, Duck Cassoulet, Grilled Pork Chops with Apple Cider Sauce, Warm Fig and Thyme Crisp

Late Harvest Viognier

In keeping with our Rhône wine list theme, Late Harvest Viognier is our dessert wine of choice. Often called the "nectar of the gods," this wine is sophisticated, elegant, luscious, and lingering. Late Harvest Viognier is an excellent accompaniment to a dessert because it pairs sugar to sugar. Viognier grapes are left on the vines for a very long time and are extremely high in sugar. Some of these wines are aged in new French oak from 15 weeks to 12 months. Because it is so sweet, a small amount of Late Harvest Viognier goes a long way. We serve a small glass to our guests.

Nose honeyed apricots and peaches
Mouthfeel lingering sweetness, velvety silk
Flavors vanilla, ripe pineapple, orange zest, apricot jam, tropical fruit, orange marmalade
Featured California producers Cambria Winery & Vineyards, Rosenblum Cellars, Andrew Murray Winery, Meredith Winery
Food pairings Meyer Lemon Tartlets with Blood Orange Sauce, Brown Butter and Almond Cake with Berries, Pear Clafouti, Lavender Crème Brûlée

Marsanne

Introducing new wines to guests who are unfamiliar with the varietals on our wine list can be a challenge. Our favorite guests view the list as a discovery about to be made. On the other hand, our most challenging guests are set in their ways and unwilling to try something new. We have a special program for this type of guest—"We know we have something you will like."

I like to think of Marsanne as a cross between a Chardonnay and a Sauvignon Blanc. Describing Marsanne as such puts guests at ease, and they will try this wine with a reference point.

There is a very limited production of Marsanne, and each year there seems to be less and less. Marsannes are generally very food friendly wines. They are good transition wines when starting with a very tart and dry wine and working your way to a full-bodied red. Marsanne bridges the two extremes quite nicely.

I love a challenge, and turning guests on to a wine that is perfectly suited for them is rewarding. We often achieve this by the process of elimination. We start by finding out what they usually drink, and then we offer two tastes of wine and ask them to select the one they prefer. If they fall in love with one right away, that's great. If not, we introduce another wine until they find one they like.

Nose honeysuckle, pears, almonds, and floral
Mouthfeel dry, crisp, rich, and luscious
Flavors pears, melon, orange rind, peaches, vanilla
Featured California producers Rosenblum Cellars, Qupé Vineyards, Beckmen Vineyards
Food pairings Carrot-Ginger Soup, Pan-Seared Scallops with Orange-Tarragon Beurre Blanc, Grilled Mahi Mahi with Tarragon Butter

Mourvèdre

I am very fond of Mourvèdre. These red grapes produce robust wines that are rich and inky and full of flavor. They should be served with a hearty meal of beans with sage, a stew of braised meats, or broccoli rabe sautéed with olive oil and garlic. They call for a cool evening with an outdoor fire blazing and a sky full of stars. These are wines to drink when celebrating with friends; every last drop should be savored.

Nose blueberry, raspberry, black cherry, leather, pipe tobacco, sage, black cherries
Mouthfeel good acidity, soft tannins
Flavors roasted meats, lavender, earth
Featured California producers Cline Cellars, Jade Mountain, Sebastiani
Food pairings Wild Mushroom Ragout, Liberty Duck Breast with Orange Pomegranate Glaze, Pan-Seared Beef Fillet with Tarragon Butter

Roussanne

Many of the wines made from Roussanne that I have had the pleasure to taste have been elegant and crisp with a heady nose of melons and honeysuckle. These white wines tend to be complex, with interesting layers of flavor. Roussanne wines age well and stand up to high-acid or herb-based sauces.

Nose honeysuckle, honey
Mouthfeel delicate, refined
Flavors bright fruit, honeysuckle, peaches, honeydew
Featured California producers Jaffurs Wine Cellars, Sobon Estate, Truchard Vineyards, Andrew Murray Vineyards
Food pairings Apricot-Cured Salmon, Shrimp and Salmon Cakes, Spring Vidalia Onion and Mushroom Soup, Grilled Fig Salad, Grilled Asparagus Salad with Lemon Thyme Vinaigrette, Lobster-Scented Risotto, Broiled Halibut with Spring Vegetable Ragout, Fig Leaf–Wrapped Rainbow Trout

Syrah

Syrah came into my life in 1997, about the same time it came into its own in California. When we first opened the girl & the fig and decided to go with a "Rhône-Alone" wine list, California Syrahs were few and far between. Today, they are a dime a dozen. Once it took hours of detective work to find quality Syrahs; now the market is oversaturated and it is difficult to select wines for our list. Why the fascination with Syrah? Wine has a cycle just as do fashion and food trends, and this is the time for Syrah.

California viticulturists and vintners realized that the hardy Syrah vines were a perfect match with most California micro-climates and terroir. Our California Pinot Noirs and Cabernet Sauvignons are similar to those from Burgundy and Bordeaux, and California has also been extremely successful in replicating the Rhône and Provençal areas in France with the Rhône varietals. Syrah wines characteristically have a marked acidity and bright, forward fruit flavors. These red wines have robust structure without being overbearing and they are graceful without being feminine.

Nose smoke, spice, tar, tobacco, sweet oak

Mouthfeel good balance, long finish, juicy acidity, layered, fleshy, long, rich, and complex, depth

Flavors earth, spice, black raspberry fruit, oak nuances, pepper

Featured California producers Alban Vineyards, Loxton Cellars, Hamel, MacRostie Winery, Ballentine Winery, Stags' Leap Winery, Culler Wines, Havens Wine Cellars, Shafer Vineyards, Unti Vineyards, Jade Mountain, Arrowood Winery

Food pairings Crispy Sweetbreads, Braised Lamb Shanks, Lamb Medallions with Syrah Reduction Sauce, Braised Beef Short Ribs, Savory Blue Cheese Soufflé with Syrah-Poached Cherries

Viognier

Although Viognier is not well known outside the wine world, of the handful of white Rhône varietals, the Viognier grape is the most popular widely grown grape in California. Because it is a difficult grape to grow, many viticulturists won't touch it. Viognier fares well in the warmer micro-climates, and as the yields are generally low, the grapes need to be picked when they are fully ripe. The Viognier grape typically doesn't respond well to the use of heavy oak or the addition of malolactic fermentation.

The white wines made from Viognier generally have flavors of ripe apricots, peaches, and figs. The aromas will be slightly sweet with a floral perfume. Though the rich aromas may indicate a sweet wine, you will find these wines to be dry, low in acidity, and full-bodied.

Nose floral, perfume, honeysuckle

Mouthfeel velvety, thick, viscous

Flavors ripe apricots, figs, peaches, orange blossoms, mangoes, roses

Featured California producers Alban Vineyards, Garretson Wine Co., Pride Mountain Vineyards, Meredith Vineyards, Foxen Vineyard, La Crema Winery, Miner Family Vineyards, Imagery Estate Winery, Equus, Jade Mountain, Arrowood Winery

Food pairings Dungeness Crab Cakes, Pernod-Scented Mussels, Cauliflower Gruyère Soup, Wild Mushroom Risotto, Braised Rabbit with Baby Artichoke Pan Sauce

seasonal menus

Spring

Spring Vidalia Onion and Mushroom Soup with Morel Croutons 74
Pan-Roasted Halibut with Caper Vinaigrette 116
Roasted Asparagus 174
Brown Butter and Almond Cake with Berries 211

Asparagus and English Pea Soup with Pistachio Butter 72
Sonoma Rabbit Two Ways with Baby Artichoke Pan Sauce 134
Basil-Scented Potato Cakes 190
Lavender and Wildflower Honey Crème Brûlée 231

Grilled Asparagus Salad with Lemon-Thyme Vinaigrette 92
Wild Mushroom Risotto 110
Cinnamon "Biscones" with Strawberries and Whipped Cream 212

Summer

Heirloom Tomato Salad with Feta and Balsamic Reduction 90
Grilled Mahi Mahi with Fire-Roasted Tomato Vinaigrette 120
Haricots Verts 173
Bellwether Farms Ricotta Cheesecake with Peaches and Cream 226

Heirloom Tomato Gazpacho 66
Shrimp and Salmon Cakes with Red Pepper Rouille 44
Roasted Asparagus 174
Profiteroles with Bittersweet Chocolate Sauce 224

Heirloom Radishes with Anchovy Butter and Sea Salt 24
Fire-Roasted Eggplant Soup 68
Pan-Roasted Sea Scallops with Orange-Tarragon Beurre Blanc 114
Warm Fig and Thyme Crisp with Fig Syrup 216

Autumn

Garden Herb Tartlet 47
Grilled Quail Salad with Hazelnut Vinaigrette 104
Mixed Nut Tart 219

Grilled Fig Salad with Fig and Port Vinaigrette 98
Grilled Pork Chops with Apple Cider Sauce 132
Apple-Yam Gratin 186
Pumpkin Cheesecake Tartlets 228

Braised Leeks 181
Grilled Chicken Breasts with Tarragon-Mustard Sauce 126
Red Chard, Cheddar, and Potato Gratin 187
Caramel Apple Tartlet with Vanilla Ice Cream 220

Winter

Potato Leek Soup 83
Braised Lamb Shanks 145
Creamy Polenta 192
Chocolate Hazelnut Tart with Frangelico Cream 222

Endive Salad with Pears and Blue Cheese with Pomegranate Vinaigrette 100
Liberty Duck Breast with Orange Pomegranate Glaze 138
Citrus Pearl Couscous 194
Chocolate Pots de Crème 234

Roasted Baby Beet and Blood Orange Salad with Champagne Vinaigrette 96
Hazelnut-and-Peppercorn-Crusted Beef Tenderloin with Syrah Reduction Sauce 152
Roasted Potatoes 188
Wilted Greens 177
Meyer Lemon Tartlets with Blood Orange Sauce 214

The Cocktail Party

Mini Dungeness Crab Cakes with Caper Aïoli 42 and 159
Mini Shrimp and Salmon Cakes with Red Pepper Rouille 44 and 162
Vella Cheese Crisps 35
Heirloom Radishes with Anchovy Butter and Sea Salt 24
Fig, Prosciutto, and Roquefort Pissaladière 49
Polenta Wedges with Pistou 43 and 161
Chicken Liver Mousse on Brioche Toast with Cornichons 51
Roasted Asparagus with Roasted Garlic Aïoli 174 and 159
Apricot-Cured Salmon with Crème Fraîche 38 and 9

the girl & the fig
the girl & the fig
fig & port
vinaigrette
8.45 fl oz/250 ml
apricot fig

the girl & the fig products

Our enthusiasm for and inspiration from figs doesn't stop at our menu items or silver fig table ornaments—we have created a line of Fig Food. Included in our fig pantry are Fig and Port Vinaigrette, Fig Balsamic Vinegar, Chocolate Fig Hazelnut Sauce, Kadota Fig Jam, Black Mission Fig Jam, Apricot Fig Chutney, and Fig and Port Syrup.

Our labels are a combination of talented artist Julie Higgins's original pastel *Figs and Phalanges* and Patti Britton's skillful graphic design. Our products, with this upbeat, colorful packaging and our delicious fig flavors, are available outside of the restaurants at select local markets and wineries. Look for new additions to our Fig Food selection!

Our signature Grilled Fig Salad is served with our Fig and Port Vinaigrette, made with Black Mission figs, port, olive oil, red wine vinegar, and shallots. Without the use of an emulsifier, our vinaigrette separates and exhibits the layers of the figs and the olive oil. A good shaking will re-blend the vinaigrette to a perfect consistency.

Create your own salad dressing or marinate pork and poultry with sweet and savory Fig Balsamic Vinegar, made with Black Mission figs and balsamic vinegar.

Our Chocolate Hazelnut Fig Sauce is a smooth blend of Callebaut chocolate, Black Mission figs, port, and toasted hazelnuts. Serve on scones or heat the sauce and dip strawberries and apricots in it for a delectable treat.

Our luscious Kadota Fig Jam is divine served with cream cheese on whole-grain toast. Use this jam on cheese platters or as a condiment for lamb and pork dishes.

Black Mission figs picked at the height of summer create our Black Mission Fig Jam, which is sweet, subtle, and delicate in flavor.

Apricot Fig Chutney is composed of plump apricots and Black Mission figs. This is a superb combination, with a hint of ginger and dried cherries. Serve this chutney with your favorite charcuterie and cheese items.

Our products are available in specialty stores and wineries in Sonoma and Napa wine country. You may also purchase these items on our website at www.thegirlandthefig.com.

Restrooms

sources

Bread

Artisan Bakers

Sonoma, California
707-939-1765
www.artisanbakers.com

Basque Boulangerie

Sonoma, California
707-935-7687

Cheese

Bellwether Farms

Petaluma, California
888-527-8606
www.bellwethercheese.com
Carmody, Crescenza, Fromage Blanc, San Andreas, Ricotta

Clover Stornetta Farms

Petaluma, California
800-237-3315
www.cloverstornettafarms.com
milk, cream, butter, eggs

Cowgirl Creamery / Tomales Bay Foods

Point Reyes Station, California
415-663-9335
www.cowgirlcreamery.com
Mt. Tam, Red Hawk, Fromage Blanc

Cypress Grove Chèvre

McKinleyville, California
707-839-3168
www.cypressgrovechevre.com
Humboldt Fog, Bermuda Triangle, Marble Mountain

Joe Matos Cheese Co.

Santa Rosa, California
707-584-5283
St. George

Laura Chenel Chèvre, Inc.

Sonoma, California
707-996-4477
Chef's Chèvre, Crottin, Fromage Blanc, Taupinière

Point Reyes Farmstead Cheese Company

Point Reyes Station, California
800-591-6878
www.pointreyescheese.com
Original Blue

Redwood Hill Farm

Sebastopol, California
707-823-8250
www.redwoodhill.com
Crottin, Camellia, Goat's Milk Cheddar

Sonoma Cheese Factory
Sonoma, California
707-996-1000
www.sonomacheese.com
Teleme

Vella Cheese Company
Sonoma, California
707-938-3232
www.vellacheese.com
Special Reserve Dry Jack

Winchester Cheese Company
Winchester, California
909-926-4239
www.winchestercheese.com
Gouda

Yerba Santa Dairy
Lakeport, California
707-263-8131
www.yerbasantadairy.com
Alpine Shepherd's Cheese

Meat, Poultry

Caggiano Company
Petaluma, California
707-765-2849
sausages, ham

Petaluma Poultry
Petaluma, California
707-763-1904
www.petalumapoultry.com
Rocky chicken, Rosie chicken

Sonoma Foie Gras
Sonoma, California
800-427-4559
www.sonomafoiegras.com
artisan foie gras

Sonoma County Poultry
Petaluma, California
800-95DUCKS
www.libertyducks.com
Liberty ducks

Pantry

Critelli Olive Oil Company
Fairfield, California
888-654-8399
www.critelli.com
extra virgin olive oil, blended oil

McEvoy Ranch
Petaluma, California
707-433-4755
www.mcevoyranch.com
extra virgin olive oil

Napa Nuts
Napa, California
707-226-6083
dried figs, nuts

Remezzano Olive Oil
Sonoma, California
www.remezzano.com
infused olive oils

The Olive Press
Glen Ellen, California
707-939-8900/800-9OLIVE9
www.theolivepress.com
olive oil, olive trees

Valley Fig Growers
Fresno, California
559-237-3893
www.valleyfig.com
dried figs every way

Produce

Greenleaf Produce Company
San Francisco, California
415-647-2991
www.greenleafsf.com
vegetables, fruit, herbs, fig leaves

Lorenc Lavender Farm
Kenwood, California
707-833-6681
www.lavendernook.com
lavender

Middleton Farm
Healdsburg, California
707-433-4755
vegetables, herbs

Oak Hill Farm
Glen Ellen, California
707-996-6643
vegetables, fruit, herbs, flowers

Sonoma Organics
Sebastopol, California
707-829-8200
www.sonomaorganics.com
vegetables, herbs

Swedes Feeds Pet & Garden
Kenwood, California
707-833-5050
plants, seeds

The Apple Farm
Philo, California
707-895-2461
organic apples, apple butter, cooking classes, mail order

Seafood

Hog Island Shellfish Company
Marshall, California
415-663-9218
www.hogislandoyster.com
oysters

Royal Hawaiian
San Francisco, California
415-824-1177
seafood, shellfish

Spirits

Bonny Doon Vineyard
Santa Cruz, California
866-666-3396
www.bonnydoonvineyard.com
Framboise

Figoun

www.liquoristerie-provence.fr

Wine

Hospice du Rhône

San Luis Obispo, California

805-784-9546

www.hospicedurhone.com

The Rhone Rangers

Sonoma, California

707-939-8014

www.rhonerangers.org

Other Food Sources

Ramekins Sonoma Valley Culinary School

Sonoma, California

www.ramekins.com

Ramekins is a combination of a cooking school and a bed and breakfast, located four blocks off historic Sonoma Plaza. Ramekins features cooking classes taught by chefs from across the country.

Copia: The American Center for Wine, Food & the Arts

Napa, California

707-259-1600

www.copia.org

Copia is many things. First and foremost it is a cultural museum that traces food and wine through history as well as an education center that offers classes, films, and concerts. Classes vary from cooking to food history to gardening to artist demonstrations and wine tastings. A visit to wine country is not complete without a tour of this very special facility.

Sonoma County Farm Trails

www.farmtrails.org

Sonoma County Farm Trails is an organization that connects the local farms with public awareness. They have an informative map available from their website that describes the local farms and seasonality and celebrates the diversity of Sonoma County.

table of equivalents*

Liquid and Dry Measures

United States	*Metric*
¼ teaspoon	1.25 milliliters
½ teaspoon	2.5 milliliters
1 teaspoon	5 milliliters
1 tablespoon (3 teaspoons)	15 milliliters
1 fluid ounce (2 tablespoons)	30 milliliters
¼ cup	65 milliliters
⅓ cup	80 milliliters
1 cup	235 milliliters
1 pint (2 cups)	480 milliliters
1 quart (4 cups, 32 ounces)	950 milliliters
1 gallon (4 quarts)	3.8 liters
1 ounce (by weight)	28 grams
1 pound	454 grams
2.2 pounds	1 kilogram

Oven Temperatures

Fahrenheit	*Celsius*	*Gas*
250	120	½
275	140	1
300	150	2
325	160	3
350	180	4
375	190	5
400	200	6
425	220	7
450	230	8
475	240	9
500	260	10

* The exact equivalents in the above tables have been rounded off for convenience.

Index

(Page numbers in *italics* refer to illustrations.)

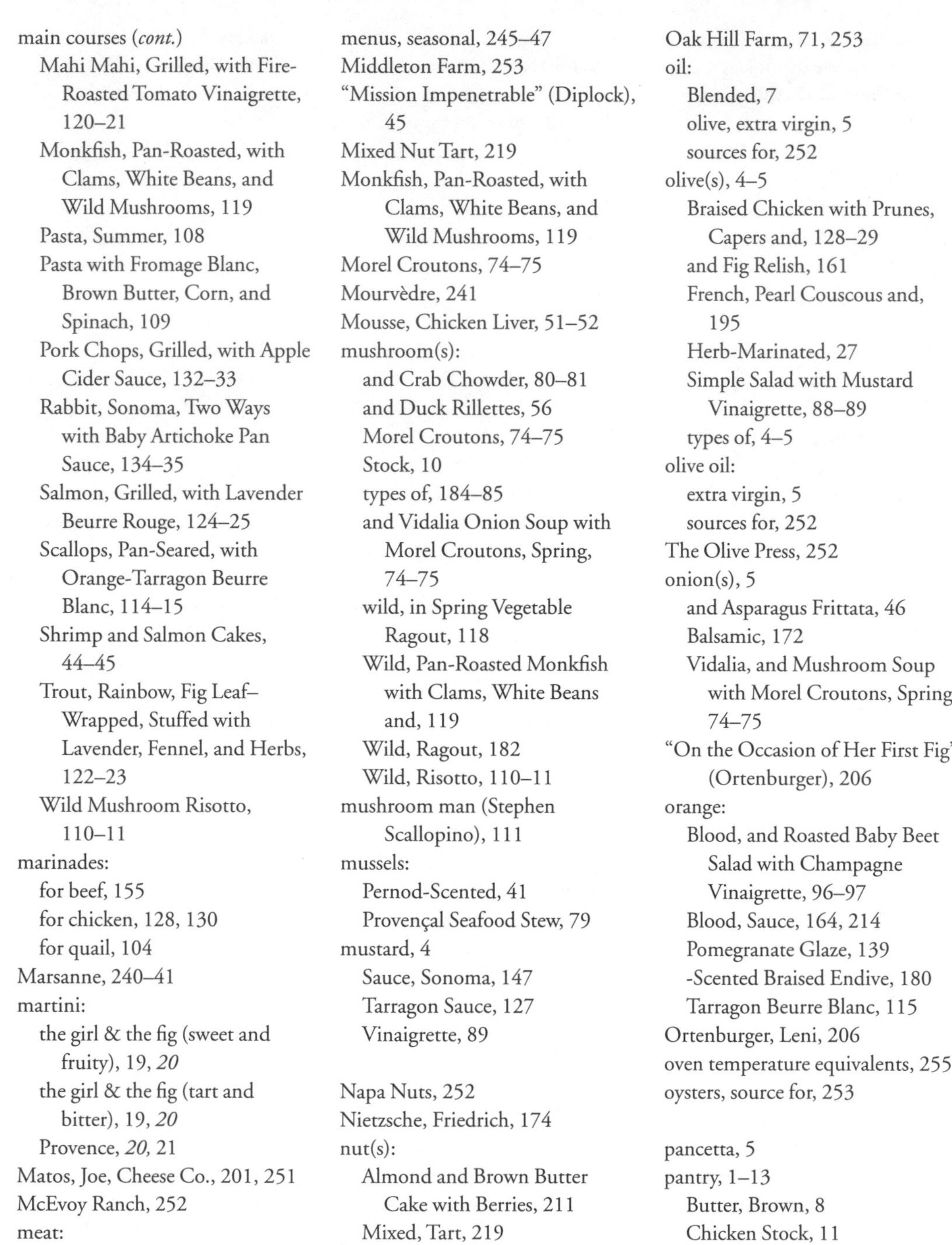